JChapin
Dec 2011

Land of the Free

A Painter's Chronicle of Our 50 States and their Heroes

Jane Chapin

Preface

Painting books are typically coffee table tributes to the artist. In 2007, when I bought a motor home and began the project of traveling across the country to paint, I might have imagined such a book. But the journey itself quickly adjusted my focus. The more ground I covered, the more I realized how blessed my life was, and how lucky I was to be born into this time and place. I fell in love with America again. The realization of my freedom on the road reawakened me to the debt I owed our veterans, past and present. I began thinking of the paintings as symbols of the land they had fought to defend. I wanted to thank those who allowed me the privilege to wander freely across this great country and do what I love.

So this painting book is really about heroes. They came from farms, towns and cities in states that had all had some history of a struggle for freedom during our country's formation. Their state histories were heroic and tragic, full of stories both funny and poignant; of mistakes made and corrected. Woven together, the states' histories are our history as a country.

The veteran's stories spanned almost 70 years and their calls to duty were very different from one other. Some volunteered, some were drafted and some just went to work in the morning and had to make a heroic choice. They had in common their desire to serve their country and the fraternity of their brothers and sisters. As I went about the work of reading about veterans from each state, I began finding stories of wounded heroes that had not just sacrificed, but had also helped others in the process of healing themselves. I was moved not only by their sacrifice, but by their indomitable will. Far from depressing, their stories were uplifting and inspired me to give this small tribute back to them.

Each page in the book represents a state and, with two exceptions, they appear in the order that they were painted. Like the order of statehood, the painting order was not linear and subject to outside events. Alaska and New Mexico, which appear near the end, were actually painted before I began my RV trip.

Each one of their pages could be a book in itself. The choice to make this as brief as it is, was intentional. The state histories are incomplete and only intended as a starting point. For every veteran whose name appears there are thousands who deserve mention. I cannot thank them all enough.

All money from the sale of these books will go to the Special Operations Warrior Foundation. Please note the charitable organizations listed throughout the book and their websites listed in the Bibliography. There are many more that also deserve our support. Please investigate any charities and give to those that use your donations wisely.

Dedication

To my parents: My first heroes, who taught me to be thankful.

My mother passed away in 2009 before this book was finished. An avid reader with an inquisitive mind, Mom loved history and never stopped learning, reading even when her vision was nearly gone. My goal was to write something she would have enjoyed. She gave me roots.

My father was a Navy pilot in World War II, flying the F4U Corsair off the carrier Antietam. Dad took me up for flights at the local airport and taught me by word and example that I could do anything I set my mind to. He gave me wings.

Maine

"And over us the wise and noble-hearted, twilight leaned down; the sunset mists were parted
And we, with thoughts on tiptoe, slunk down the green, twisting alleys of the Kennebunk"

-Magic

Louis Untermeyer

Revolutionary Beginnings

Maine is where my 50 state journey began before I even knew it was beginning. I've loved Maine ever since my parents piled three of us in the back seat of a '54 Ford for the long trip up US 11 from Pennsylvania. I moved there in my twenties and had my two children there during the 7 years when I had no spare money or time to paint those scenic surroundings. So, in the fall of 2007 when I was invited to paint a croquet tournament on Mount Desert Island, I happily accepted. I packed up my cat and my dog and joyously drove my new camper up Route 1 to Penobscot Bay and Acadia National Park. The tournament players in their crisp whites against the backdrop of the blue waters inspired me to extend my stay. Meeting up with some friends, we headed to Cushing to paint in Andrew Wyeth country and I chose to paint his favorite hay wagon. I camped in Camden Hills and watched the ships moving through the bay, painting them several times during the week.

'DOWN EAST' The expression has origins in the sailing world when ships would sail to Maine from Massachusetts, using the prevailing westerlies, sailing downwind to go northeast.

Maine has a rich naval and shipbuilding history. The first naval battle of the Revolution was fought "down east" in Machias Bay in 1775.

Then part of Massachusetts, the people of Machias heard about the battles of Lexington & Concord and did not want their lumber used to build barracks for occupying British forces, even though the goods to be traded were desperately needed supplies. In defiance of the king, they erected a liberty pole in the town square, prompting the British ship 'Margaretta' to threaten an assault upon the town. Armed with more pitchforks than guns, forty townspeople aboard the sloop 'Unity' defeated the armed British schooner. As I left Maine and headed west on Route 2, I became inspired to paint our great nation one state at a time.

Bill Knight of Bangor served in the Army Air Corps in WWII. With a total of 32 years in the military, he took part in the mission to keep Rommel pinned down in northern Africa. At 88 and battling cancer, he still serves with many other veterans and citizens as a troop greeter at Bangor International Airport, the easternmost point for deploying and returning troops. No matter the hour, members of all branches of the U.S. military are assured a handshake, use of a free cell phone and a snack as they pass through. Over a million troops have been served by this volunteer organization. "The Way We Get By," a film about *the Maine Troop Greeters* featuring Knight, won 24 awards.[1]

New Hampshire

"...up in the Mountains of New Hampshire, God Almighty has hung out a sign to show that there He makes men."

Daniel Webster

Faith, Hope and Charity

I followed Route 2 west leaving Maine and crossing into Shelburne, New Hampshire. Amid the spectacular scenery of the White Mountains, the campground owner directed me to the Shelburne Union Church as a possible painting site. The late afternoon sun was lighting up the fall leaves on the mountains in the background and casting wonderful long shadows from the old church, so I had to work quickly.

The town itself was first settled in 1771 by farmers who moved west from Maine. The account of one of the first settlers can be found in the limited historical records of Shelburne. **Hope** *Austin built a wood shelter with a pine bough roof before his wife and 3 children walked through 5 foot snows from present day Gorham to spend their first winter. Shortly after, they added a more secure structure to protect them from the weather and wild animals.*

The town was named for the Earl of Shelburne, William Petty Fitzmaurice, who was an advocate for the American colonies. When they incorporated in 1820, they decided to keep the name in his honor. The church originally was constructed by people of **faith** *in 1832, then torn down and rebuilt at its current location in 1885. It recently had benefitted from a restoration effort funded by the* **charity** *of area residents and visitors and is now able to be used for services during the summer months. Leaving town the following day, I passed an incredible grove of birch trees and paused to sit in the filtered sunlight by a clear running river. I later read it was dedicated to Shelburne's soldiers who had served in World War II and became a very popular spot for artists and photographers.*

A 1982 plane crash - while he was serving in Alaska with the Coast Guard - paralyzed Chris Devlin-Young below the waist. Following the crash, he discovered skiing and racing at the first Veterans Administration Winter Sports Clinic. Devlin-Young has won 51 medals in world competitions, was named Disabled Skier of the Year by Ski Racing magazine in 2003, 2004, 2007, 2008 and 2009. In keeping with his personal promise to give back, he coached the first race development camp for disabled veterans. He has dedicated himself "to learning all I can about disabled skiing and teaching that knowledge to others." He is the founder of the *New England Disabled Ski Team* and resides in Campton.[2]

Vermont

"If ever the spirit of liberty should vanish from the rest of the Union, it could be restored by the generous share held by the people in this brave little State of Vermont."

Calvin Coolidge

Who is Joe?

On Route 2 between Maine and Montpelier, I could paint for weeks - around every turn is a street or a farm or a lake where I would have liked to stop. This barn caught my eye near Joe's Pond in Danville, Vermont. Joe's Pond was named for Indian Joe, a child of the Abernaki tribe, a branch of the Algonquin. At the age of six he was left an orphan when the British took Louisburg and fled with the remaining tribe to St Francis, Quebec. During the French and Indian War, Joe was taken on a raid party to Vermont, somewhere near Newbury. The Indians were driven off by the white men, with the exception of Joe, who was left behind badly wounded. Taken care of by a white family near Danville, Joe pledged to warn them of future Indian attacks. He stayed in the area rather than return to Canada as a British territory. Losing his family made him a lifelong enemy of the British. He became a Revolutionary scout for the Americans, eventually becoming an outcast to his own people.

After the Revolution ended, Indian Joe received a letter of appreciation from General George Washington himself. It summoned Joe to Washington's headquarters at Newburgh, on the Hudson. Joe and his wife made the trip by canoe and on foot. He was always very proud of his visit with Washington. So beloved is his legacy that Danville must share it with the nearby towns of Walden, Derby, Newbury and Cabot who also claim him.

An American of Sioux descent, Mark Andrade of Ludlow, received injuries when serving in the 101st Airborne in 1989. Years later his injuries resulted in his 100 percent disability. While in Florida for pain treatment, he acquired a horse which had been beaten and partially blinded by her owner. He bonded with the horse and enrolled in a training course for disabled riders. In a wheelchair, Andrade sometimes has seizures and if he falls off she is trained to stand over him and drag him off the road if necessary. Moving back to Ludlow, Andrade and 'Jersey Girl' give rides to disabled children. "I can't describe it, the magic in a kid's eyes. It's a good feeling for me, but it's a better feeling for Jersey."[3]

9

"Lake George is without comparison, the most beautiful water I ever saw... its water limpid as crystal and the mountainsides covered with rich groves of silver fir."

Thomas Jefferson

The Element of Surprise

I left Vermont crossing Lake Champlain on a beautiful late afternoon ferry ride and arrived after dark in Lake George. Heavy morning fog cancelled my plan to paint by the lake. I went back to pack up the camper and had just decided to paint New York another day when I looked out the front window and saw the scene right in front of me. There was a young girl at the pop up camper next door and the sunlight had just come out catching the edges of their camper and the American flag. I quickly set up and started painting. After about 45 minutes I was "discovered" by the family. I told them about my new project and Dad Scott and his two kids were quite happy to represent their state. From Poughkeepsie, they were on their way to be a chase crew for the balloon festival in Lake George. Since they were in a hurry, I promised to email a photo of the finished painting. I would find out two years later that Scott was a Purple Heart veteran.

The previous night I had passed Ticonderoga in the near dark. It had a strategic location at the north of Lake George overlooking the British invasion route from Canada, down Lake Champlain to the Hudson Valley. Fort Ticonderoga was the first American victory of the Revolution when Ethan Allen and the Green Mountain Boys seized it in a surprise night raid from the British without a single loss of life. Colonel Allen gave his overconfident account of the ease of the victory when he went to the British commander's quarters, "...the Captain came immediately to the door, with his britches in his hand, when I ordered him to deliver me the fort instantly."

In July 2004, Kevin Workman was mobilized overseas as a National Guardsman. He was in a Humvee turret when his convoy was attacked. In what his lieutenant would call "an amazing act of courage" Workman's defense of the convoy was credited with saving lives. The force of the blast caused him traumatic brain injuries which would remain undiagnosed for some time. He was unable to return to his civilian job with the State Police in South Carolina, and was medically retired out of the Army in 2008. An avid hunter and outdoorsman prior to the war, he opened *Liberty Lodge Outfitters* at his home in Locke to give an outdoor retreat to wounded soldiers, police and firefighters.[4]

Pennsylvania

"Nowhere in this country, from sea to sea, does nature comfort us with such assurance of plenty, such rich and tranquil beauty as in those unsung, unpainted hills of Pennsylvania."

Rebecca Harding Davis

Going Home

The barn in this painting was just outside of Danville, Pennsylvania – about 30 minutes from my hometown. It is such an ordinary little scene, so familiar that I must have passed one like it thousands of times without even looking up to notice. But when I think of Pennsylvania, this is what comes to mind, not Independence Hall, Ben Franklin, Gettysburg or any of those great historic references that are so rich in my home state.

We grew up calling it the "Keystone State" and knew that reference to the supporting stone in an arch meant our state had been vital to the structure of the new nation. But our citizens' connection to the state had more to do with the land itself than its

We get too soon old and too late smart.
- Pennsylvania Dutch proverb

meaning to the union. For that, we owe William Penn, who avoided selling the land to the large landowners and gentry of the southern colonies and instead leased it to yeoman farmers. Penn also insisted on paying the native Americans for the land, thus fostering good relations between the tribes and settlers. Slavery existed in the state, but died early on, both due to moral objections by the large Quaker population and the economics of the small farmers. Immigrant Germans came willingly as indentured servants and eventually became a large part of the farming community themselves.

By the time of the Revolution, there were over 100,000 Germans or "Pennsylvania Dutch" and their imprint on the state is still very visible today. The various farming populations, including the Amish and Mennonites, retain their way of life as well as the legacy of beautiful farm scenes for all of us to come home to.

Before leaving Pennsylvania, I stopped at Shanksville to see the *Flight 93 Memorial*, reminded of the heroism of ordinary citizens. Deborah Anne Jacobs Welsh, flight attendant and a Darby native, was not originally slated to be on Flight 93 but was assigned to the flight when she swapped shifts. Relatives dubbed her "The Little Apostle of the Airlines" after discovering that she often left Newark airport with a stack of unused airline meals to hand out to homeless people on the streets of Hell's Kitchen, her adopted New York City neighborhood.[5]

West Virginia

"Fair were our visions! Oh, they were grand

As ever floated out of faerie land:

Children were we in single faith,

But God-like children, whom nor death

Nor threat nor danger drove from honor's path"

-In the Land Where We Were Dreaming

Daniel B. Lucas

14

Almost Heaven, Westsylvania

I stopped to paint the fall colors at Coopers Rock State Park in northern West Virginia and stayed at a nearby campground. The next day it was raining so I elected to travel on the Interstate for the first part of the trip, getting on the back roads when I saw the sky lighten to the east. I traveled down route 219 from Elkins, surprised at how great the road was. What a beautiful mountainous state West Virginia is! Finding no campgrounds for my second night, I had my first and only parking lot camping experience in Lewisburg and slept to the hum of several nearby generators.

West Virginia was one of only two states formed during the Civil War and the only one to secede from the Confederacy. The western counties of pre Civil War Virginia were different geographically and culturally than the east. Named "Westsylvania" in a 1776 petition to form a separate state, a large part of the population emigrated from Pennsylvania, much of it German. The rugged geography made slavery unprofitable for the western counties and many shared their northern neighbors' Quaker heritage. Over the years their separation only increased, until 1861, when they voted for secession. West Virginia was finally admitted to the Union as a separate state in 1863. Disputes over financial debts and the exact location of borders would continue into the late 1900's.

Marine Dan O'Connor, St. Albans, was injured in Vietnam when his right leg was shattered by a "Bouncing Betty" mine. A former high school cross country runner, he could not run on his leg even after 14 surgeries. In 2005 a motorcycle accident cost him his left leg, but gave him back his activity. While attending an amputee conference in Atlanta, O'Connor met wounded veterans from the *Achilles Track Club Freedom Team* and they invited him to join. Using aerodynamic hand cranked wheel chairs, they compete in marathons across the country. O'Connor, 63, says he is in the best shape of his life and wants to complete in 100 marathons by the time he is 70. He is a peer counselor with the *Amputee Coalition of America.* O'Connor says he would not reverse losing his leg, "This way, I get to help our wounded vets."[6]

North Carolina

"I confess that in 1901 I said to my brother Orville that man would not fly for fifty years."

Wilbur Wright

Paris on the river

Leaving Lynchburg, Virginia I drove south through the rain to North Carolina, glad I did not have much distance to cover. As soon as the rain let up, I left the Interstate and headed south to Route 64. I got to my campground in the late afternoon and lucked onto a lakefront site. The rain ended and the next day I found two beautiful little canoes by the lake. While I was painting, a group of children stopped to watch. One of them asked me to paint her - her name was Paris and she was named after "some perfume her grandmother liked." I did a small painting and gave it to her after she very politely let me know my painting prices were "a little ridiculous."

The campground was along the Yadkin, a river as long and winding as its history. Northwest on the river is Shallow Ford, a river crossing that was a major route for early settlers from Pennsylvania, bringing Daniel Boone's family to reside in nearby Mocksville. The river was a troop and supply route during the Revolution with a key battle that took place at Shallow Ford.

Eighty five years later, during the Civil War, the river was once again a highway for troops and supplies. With many telegraphs destroyed, the river became the primary communication route, although the delay in news was costly. On April 9, 1865 Lee surrendered at Appomattox unbeknownst to the soldiers in the field. On the same day, the Union army was marching down the river to Salisbury. Five days later, while Salisbury was still smoldering, news of Abraham Lincoln's assassination had yet to reach the battlefield.

"I believe there's a silver lining to everything," says Cpl John Hyland of Charlotte. "Events in our lives happen for a reason."
Cpl. Hyland joined the Army when he was 33 years old and trained for an elite position as a scout. On a mission near Baghdad in 2007, Hyland's vehicle set off two anti-tank bombs. The blast crushed his feet and fractured bones in his back and pelvis. Despite 33 operations, Hyland still had his lower left leg amputated. A struggling opera singer before joining the Army, he was invited to sing the national anthem at the Coca Cola 600 in Charlotte. "I'm proud to represent the Army, my country, my family, Charlotte and all of the wounded soldiers out there."[7]

South Carolina

"I was born and raised on a Carolina sea island and I carried the sunshine of the low-country, inked in dark gold, on my back and shoulders."
-- *The Prince of Tides*   Pat Conroy

A Flood of Memories

With relatives in South Carolina, I had spent quite a bit of time in the southern and "low country" end of the state. Exploring the northwestern corner on this trip, I camped at Lake Hartwell. I walked down to the water to paint a late afternoon view, the red clay banks showing the severe drought. Overlooking the lake, I had no idea of the history 100 feet below its surface.

Fort Prince George was built in 1753 in the Cherokee village of Keowee on the banks of the river of the same name. In exchange for the Cherokee's allegiance, the fort was given to the tribe by the British for protection during the perilous times leading up to the French and Indian War. However, there were numerous accounts of British mistreatment of their warriors and in retaliation, the Cherokee raided British settlements. The British took over the fort, eventually resulting in the killing of the commander and the massacre of the 29 Indian hostages. With their village, livestock and crops destroyed, The Cherokee ceded northwestern South Carolina to the colony at the end of the Cherokee War in 1761. Following the treaties, 3 Cherokee chiefs were invited to tour London and meet with King George. In sympathy with the chiefs following the hostilities at the fort, the British issued the Royal Proclamation of 1763, prohibiting settlement west of the Mississippi. The proclamation became one of the major irritants leading to the Revolution.

In 1968, archeologists would uncover the fort as well as the skeleton of the fort's commander. They would have a short time to resurrect the history before the land was flooded by 18,500 acres of water in building the Keowee Dam. Today Lake Keowee, along with Lake Jocassee and Hartwell cover what was once the Cherokee's fertile valley.

Stacy L. Pearsall got her start as an Air Force combat photographer at the age of 17. During three tours in Iraq, she earned the Bronze Star Medal and Commendation with Valor for heroic actions under fire. Sergeant Pearsall incurred injuries that led to partial hearing loss and neurological problems. Repeated IED explosions resulted in nerve damage that caused numbness and pain, but she still competed in the 2010 Warrior Games. Her portrayal of combat experiences in Iraq, "Inside an Ambush," was published in News Photographer, the National Press Photographers Association's magazine in 2007. She is the only woman to win NPPA's Military Photographer of the Year twice. She runs her own photography business in Charleston.[8]

Georgia

"Out of the hills of Habersham,
Down the valleys of Hall,
I hurry amain to reach the plain,
Run the rapid and leap the fall. "

~ *Song of the Chattahoochee*
Sidney Lanier

Church and State

Crossing into Georgia at Lake Hartwell, I traveled down Routes 17 and 78 past some beautiful farmland on the road to Augusta. I followed signs to the historic district and St. Paul's Church. After wandering the grounds and reading the historical markers, I began to look for a painting subject. A gate at the front of the church was beautifully backlit and caught my attention.

This site on the Savannah River was originally selected as a trading post. In 1735, General Oglethorpe built Fort Augusta, maintaining a garrison there until 1767. The fort was the meeting place where chiefs of the Cherokee, Creek, Catawba, Chickasaw and the Choctaw along with governors of Georgia, North and South Carolina and Virginia and the King's representative signed a peace treaty. It was here that the Cherokee ceded the eastern lands which were mentioned on the South Carolina page. During the Revolution, the British erected Fort Cornwallis on the grounds. The Celtic cross on the grounds today commemorates the original fort.

On a later trip through the state, I visited the Civil War Naval Museum in Columbus. It houses many artifacts and maintains an excellent account of Naval History. I had never realized how big a role the Navy played in the Civil War from blockades of supply routes to point blank range river battles. In addition to the blue water and green water navy classifications of the oceans, there was the brown water navy of the inland rivers. Although less prestigious as an officer appointment, their river battles were critical to the war.

Scott Winkler, 35, of Augusta, was injured in Tikrit in 2003 in a truck accident that left him a paraplegic. "For a long time I went through a lot of depression," Winkler said. "Finally I said, 'Enough is enough.' "

He attended a Paralympics summer camp in Colorado Springs in 2006 and tried a number of different sports, finally settling on the shot put. In 2007, he set a world adaptive shot put record at the *U.S. Paralympics* National Championships. At the Beijing Olympics in 2008, he set a personal best at 11.27 meters, finishing 5th.

"I love my country. I'd die for my country as a soldier, now I want to win for my country as an athlete."[9]

Florida

"Florida was to Americans what America had always been to the rest of the world —
a fresh, free, unspoiled start."
-- *The Orchid Thief*   Susan Orlean

Of Mice and Mullet...and Moons: Exploration and Discovery

Florida became my new permanent home in 1994 and I have probably painted more of it than any other state. The painting of the fishing boats was done in the historic fishing village of Cortez, on the Intracoastal Waterway in Sarasota Bay. Contrary to popular belief, there are such beings as native Floridians and you are almost guaranteed to meet some in Cortez. Named for the Spanish explorer, this little town full of colorful cottages has tenaciously resisted being 'discovered' by the development on most of Florida's coast.

Fishermen from North Carolina settled in Hunter's Point on Sarasota Bay, during the land boom in 1881. They salt packed the plentiful mullet for shipment to Cuba. Then the advent of ice packing grew the small business into a major fishing operation between Hunter's Point and Tampa. When the small fishing village became large enough to have a post office, someone changed its name to Cortez, perhaps not realizing they named it for an explorer who had never set foot in Florida.

After Ponce de Leon and DeSoto explored Florida, and Spain had dominated the region for over two centuries, they traded the land to the British in exchange for Cuba in 1763. Spain regained Florida after the Revolution, offering land grants to large numbers of American settlers. They ceded it to the US in 1821 and the new territory brought southern plantation owners and the formal arrival of slavery. The native Seminole and Miccosukee tribes took in refugee slaves which became intolerable to plantation owners. Some Native Americans were forcibly relocated to Oklahoma while others were driven south into the Everglades.

During the Civil War, Florida joined the Confederacy and controlled the interior of the state while the Union Navy controlled the coastal ports, beginning the separate influences that would continue long after. The interior of Florida became agricultural while tourists flocked to the coasts. Finally in the 1960's a famous mouse discovered some swamp land near Orlando while men explored the moon from a sandy stretch of land called the Space Coast.

Jason Havlik of Jacksonville discovered his calling after serving in the military for 12 years. He then went back to Iraq as a private contractor to train Iraqi police. He returned in 2009 after a friend lost both of his legs when an IED hit his vehicle. Havlik planned an off-roading trip to Texas to help his buddy have some fun. When other wounded vets joined in, Havlik began *Wheelers for the Wounded,* an off-roading tour that makes a one on one connection with wounded veterans.[10]

Alabama

"Rising out of the ground like a swamp mist

And falling out of heaven like soft dew"

~ Daybreak in Alabama

Langston Hughes

My Mobile Mansion

As I left the Florida Panhandle, storms were building up, bringing strong winds with threats of tornados and hail, so I got off at the first exit in Alabama. The first RV Park was called Hilltop and that's exactly where it was. It would have been good to have one called 'Valley' given the forecast. But it was a nice place with no trees to fall on anything so I settled in until the storms completely cleared out. Fortunately we only got strong winds, the severe weather passing to the north. A yellow ribbon on a house just down the road reminded me of the journey ahead. It was a short drive to Mobile where I got directions to the Garden district. I drove down lovely tree lined streets absolutely convinced that one of those branches was going to claim my air conditioner, but I arrived in one piece at Oakleigh House and got permission to paint.

James W. Roper made his fortune in Mobile and dreamed of building a Greek temple in an oak grove. That dream was realized with Oakleigh in 1833. Alfred Irwin came to Mobile as secretary of the Mobile and Ohio Railroad in the late 1840s and eventually purchased Oakleigh in 1852. During the Union occupation of Mobile, Margaret Irwin saved the house from occupation or damage by draping a British flag on the front gallery. The Irwins occupied the house through the Golden Era of Mobile. They were leading lights of Mobile society, entertaining family, friends, neighbors, writers, actors, artists and a future president. In 1877, future U.S. President James Garfield sipped his first genuine Southern mint julep on Oakleigh's front gallery as a guest of the T.K. Irwins. In 1955, Oakleigh became Mobile's Official Period House Museum.

Army Sgt. Sophia Malone, Huntsville, began her military career at age 19 in Operation Desert Storm, becoming the fifth generation of military service in her family. She left the military for 9 years to marry and have three children, and then rejoined the National Guard as a truck commander in a force with the primary mission to train Iraqi police. She suffered neck and shoulder injuries when her Humvee was struck by an IED. During recuperation, the Purple Heart veteran continues to serve as a human resources administrative assistant at Space and Missile Defense Command, awaiting her return to duty with the 128th. "I wasn't the only one in a truck that got blown up." she said. "You do your job and keep going."[11]

Louisiana

The whole of Louisiana flows through New Orleans. Not only do the network of rivers, lakes and canals physically flow into it, but the history of all points north on the Mississippi is tied directly to their southernmost port. Control of the port was the main reason for the Louisiana Purchase and the 13 states whose land was acquired in that deal owe their beginning to New Orleans.

Flowing into the delta as well was a myriad of cultural influences that distilled down to a unique brew of people, language and music.

The cultural mix that built the city still gives it its character. If I was to paint Louisiana, I had to paint in New Orleans.

"Louisiana in September was like an obscene phone call from nature. The air moist, sultry, secretive"

- Jitterbug Perfume   Tom Robbins

The Battle for New Orleans

The I-10 causeway across Lake Pontchartrain was long and very rough, slowing me to 35 mph in places. The road felt like an old wooden roller coaster track. The sheer size of the body of water I was crossing made the idea of a levee holding it back seem impossible. The city is divided by I-10: Lake Pontchartrain and the low lying areas to the north; the Mississippi River and the higher ground of the French Quarter, Garden District and Central Business District to the south. In 2005 the eventuality happened when flooding overtook the levees and the word Katrina became permanently attached to the city. I was happy to learn that a word does not define New Orleans and that history has seen it overcome much greater challenges.

A quiet painting spot in the French Quarter is a rare commodity but on the eastern boundary is an exception - Esplanade Avenue. What began as a portage trade route between the lake and the Mississippi River, it saw Native American traders, then settlers from France and Spain trace the path. It was the home of "Millionaire's Row" when New Orleans was the wealthiest city in the US and not coincidentally also the largest slave trading market. Yet it was also once famed for its large educated free black population. They fought side by side along with Creoles, Anglos and pirates during the last battle of the War of 1812. Troops moved along the avenue when Andrew Jackson led an outnumbered, poorly equipped army and beat impossible odds to protect the city against the British siege in the Battle of New Orleans. Esplanade became a wide shady street where Edgar Degas lived during his time painting in New Orleans. 135 years later, I found a shady spot of my own and painted a couple discovering the city.

J.R. Martinez, Shreveport, enlisted in the United States Army in September 2002. He was deployed to Iraq in February and in April 2003, J.R. was serving as a driver of a Humvee when his left front tire hit a landmine. He suffered severe burns to more than 40 percent of his body. After 32 surgeries, Martinez was hired as an actor in 2008, using his experience to portray an injured veteran on "All My Children." Also a motivational speaker, Martinez was the 2009 recipient of the *Iraq and Afghanistan Veterans of America* Leadership Award.[12]

Mississippi

"The broad, unhasting river flows, spotted with rain-drops, gray with night;

Upon its curving breast there goes, a lonely steamboat's larboard light"

-On the Mississippi   Hamlin Garland

A Trace of History

I got off the interstate to head up Dylan's famous Highway 61 to Natchez, Mississippi. The campground was just across the river in Vidalia, Louisiana. On Easter Sunday I drove back to Natchez to paint a riverboat on the Mississippi. After having a solo Easter dinner of chicken, cornbread stuffing and green beans, I got on the Natchez Trace parkway for a scenic trip through history.

I love surprises. I happened across the Natchez Trace brochure in the welcome center, and decided it looked too good to miss. I also love to learn about history and this 444 mile route has plenty. It is believed to have started as animal paths, and was used by hunters from the Choctaw and Chickasaw tribes. By the 1700's it was used by explorers like DeSoto. In the 1800's it was traveled by settlers, slaves, traders, armies and thieves. At present, it welcomes tourists and a few RV explorers.

Today's parkway followed the route between Natchez and Nashville. I dry camped for the evening at mile 54, Rocky Springs. The remnants of the town of Rocky Springs are at the top of the hill. There were once 2600 inhabitants in what now looks like a rocky wooded path and it felt amazing to walk the same ground. Large parts of the old trace are still very intact and very hikeable. Reminders of the history are frequent and varied and I highly recommend at least a short trip on it. The sacrifices made by those who traveled that route were incredible. A simple injury - even a broken leg - could have been a death sentence. It is a reminder that many things we take for granted are a consequence of many years of sacrifice by those who came before us. As I was leaving a picnic area at mile 159, a herd of wild boars took off into the trees, about half of them babies. I had never seen them in the wild and was glad I had not seen them when walking the dog the night before.

While serving with the 155th Brigade Combat Team, Norris Galatas of Jackson was wounded by an IED blast on April 19, 2005. After more than 19 surgeries, he is still recovering. In her book *"A Soldier's Courage,"* his wife Janis tells of his bravery; from alert, through mobilization and from the battlefield of Iraq through the even greater ordeal to live and heal. She says, "He is My Hero." Proceeds from her book go to *WebofSupport.com*, a network for donors to "adopt" active duty soldiers and send them gift boxes.[13]

Arkansas

"He came from the cotton fields of Arkansas, where he had known only hard work in the sun and such emotional adventures as farm boys have on Saturday nights and Sunday afternoons."

-- "One Arm"

Tennessee Williams

Cloudy with a Chance of Vapors

Leaving Nashville and the Natchez Trace, I drove through the rain to Memphis, dashing out an unsatisfying painting in the campground. I almost changed my plan to go to Arkansas due to the forecast. The news predicted rivers cresting and more rain on the way. The Mississippi was flooded but I decided to continue, staying on the interstate to avoid problems. On a previous trip through Arkansas without my paints, the weather had been perfect and I had traveled through the scenic Ozarks. This trip took me to the south so I followed Route 70 to Hot Springs to camp in the National Park. It was a beautiful site with a waterfall right out my back window – I rested and hoped for paintable weather the following day.

Native American tribes had been gathering in the valley for over 8,000 years to enjoy the springs. The tribes agreed that they would put aside their weapons while in the valley and share the healing waters in peace. Hernando DeSoto was the first European to see what Native Americans referred to as the Valley of the Vapors when he and his men reached the area in 1541. In 1803, the springs became part of the Louisiana Purchase. Shortly after Arkansas became a territory, Hot Springs was set aside as a public reservation.

I decided to go a little more southwest the next day since the weather was still cloudy. I was chasing clear skies but never really caught them, and finally decided to paint a quick pasture scene, adding some of my own sun. I stopped for the night in DeQueen, just a few miles from the Oklahoma border.

Kevin Pannell, Dierks, was severely wounded in an ambush when two grenades exploded at his feet in 2004. Through the heroic efforts of the men of C Company, Kevin was given life-saving first aid and evacuated. After 13 operations, he recovered from his critical condition but lost both legs as a result of his wounds. He has worked as a mentor and counselor for amputee veterans in Arkansas. Today, he is an active athlete and Director of Adaptive Sports for the *Oregon Active Foundation*, helping disabled youth through sports activity.[14]

Texas

"Texas has yet to learn
submission to any oppression,
come from what source it may."

Sam Houston

Don't Mess with Texas

Despite leaving the hail storm and tornado warnings in Arkansas, my plans to paint in Oklahoma changed when the morning skies looked a threatening midnight blue. Leaving Oklahoma for another trip, I headed straight to San Antonio to visit another painter friend. Conditions improved as I went south and the following morning, the sun peeked out as I drove to San Jose Mission. The mission dates to 1721 and was a community of over 300 and one of the strongest of the mission communities. It is located on the banks of the San Antonio River four miles to the south of the earlier mission, San Antonio de Valero (the Alamo). The Spanish missions were built as a toehold against French encroachment and to spread Christianity to the native population. They were to be built no closer together than seven miles. After San Jose was built, its short distance from the Alamo was justified by measuring the distance along the twisting banks of the San Antonio River rather than the four miles over land.

'Alamo', the Spanish word for 'cottonwood' was named for the Spanish Army's base in Coahuila, Mexico. During Mexico's Revolution, it was alternately occupied by Spanish, Mexican and Rebel forces until it was taken by the Texas Revolution in 1835. The Alamo remains a symbol of a heroic struggle against impossible odds where a small band of Texans held out for thirteen days against the centralist army of General Antonio López de Santa Anna. Although the Alamo fell in the early morning hours of March 6, 1836, the death of the Alamo Defenders has come to symbolize courage and sacrifice for the cause of Liberty. The memories of James Bowie, David Crockett, and William B. Travis, are as powerful today as when the Texan Army under Sam Houston shouted "Remember the Alamo!" as it routed Santa Anna at the battle of San Jacinto on April 21, 1836.

Dr. Stanley S. McGowen (FR right) served two tours in the Army, beginning in 1969 in Vietnam. During his second 10 year tour, a 1990 airplane crash left him blind. Undeterred, he went back to school and got his PhD in American History, became a professor, published three books and 30 articles. As the National Outreach Director for the Friends of American Heroes, McGowan coordinates with Texas VA hospitals and local clubs to arrange hunting outings for veterans and disabled people. In 2007, The Armed Forces Foundation unanimously selected him as its Volunteer of the Year for his work with the Texas Project.[15]

Tennessee

"The dry and exalted noise of the locusts from all the air at once enchants my eardrums."
~Knoxville summer 1915

James Agee

A Little Country Music and a Soft Pillow

On my previous trips through Nashville and Memphis, I had spent some rainy days giving in to the lure of the tour, visiting Opryland and the Ryman in Nashville complete with embarrassing photos. I wanted to paint at Tootsie's or one of the downtown music bars that have so much history, but weather was not on my side. Moving on to Graceland, I asked for permission to paint on the grounds but was turned down. I took the tour anyway as Paul Simon sang "for reasons I cannot explain." I was never an Elvis fan but there were two

things that surprised me: how ordinary the house was and how extraordinary Elvis was – something very decent and sad about him that comes through on the tour. I did a little painting of some Bradford pear trees in the Graceland campground. But thinking that Tennessee deserved another look, on my second visit I stopped to paint a cabin in Fort Donelson.

Fort Donelson was a decisive battle in the Civil War due to a huge miscalculation from Confederate General Pillow. In the initial attacks the Union forces had been soundly defeated and Pillow withdrew 2000 troops to Nashville, thinking the threat was over. (During the battlefield presentation, there were numerous puns about Pillow being too "soft") General Grant regrouped in a vigorous attack and cut off the remaining Confederate troops' escape route. After this vital battle the South was forced to give up southern Kentucky and much of Tennessee. The Tennessee and Cumberland Rivers, and railroads in the area, became vital Federal supply lines. Also from this battle, Grant was given the nickname "Unconditional Surrender Grant", a promotion and subsequent victories that would eventually take him all the way to the White House.

Sonia Meneses, Clarksville, is a 12-year Army veteran. Originally from Azores, Portugal, she moved to the United States at the age of 13. After high school, Sonia enlisted in the Army and began working as a heavy wheeled vehicle operator. Repeated exposure to weapons fire and explosions caused significant hearing loss and loss of consciousness, eventually requiring medical evacuation from Iraq and a diagnosis of Ménière's Disease. Meneses was awarded a full-time Fellowship from *The Mission Continues* to serve as a volunteer and mentor at *Big Brothers Big Sisters* of Clarksville. [16]

Kentucky

"...us Kentucky girls, we have fire and ice in our blood. We can ride horses, be a debutante, throw left hooks, and drink with the boys, all the while making sweet tea, darlin'. And if we have an opinion, you know you're gonna hear it."

Ashley Judd

Five Dollar Deal

Land between the Lakes is a recreational area shared by Kentucky and Tennessee. The rivers feeding the lakes are the Cumberland on the east and Tennessee on the west. The sister fort of Donelson is Fort Henry. While the fort itself is in Tennessee, much of the battle to secure the two waterways was on the opposite shore in Kentucky.

In addition to the dog and cat who have been my usual travel companions, my husband Roger joined me on this trip which will take us to the west coast and back. He enjoyed reading up on the area's history while I stopped to paint in Hillman's Ferry on the Tennessee River side of the peninsula. Later we stopped for lunch in Paducah before heading west.

Paducah was originally called Pekin, a mixed community of Chickasaw and settlers attracted by the confluence of rivers. According to legend, Chief Paduke had his counsel lodge on Island Creek and welcomed the people traveling down the Ohio and Tennessee on flatboats. The settlers respectfully settled across the creek and the two communities lived in harmony until William Clark of the Lewis and Clark Expedition arrived with a title deed. Because the deed was issued by the US Supreme Court, the Chief and the settlers gave little resistance when Clark asked them to move. The deed cost only $5.00 to process, but carried with it the full authority of the U. S. Government backed by the United States Army. In exchange, Clark named his newly acquired lands after the chief.

Sgt. Robbie Doughty of Paducah lost both legs to a mortar blast in Iraq in 2004, ending a 10 year Army career. Only four months after the attack, he said, "I'll try to figure out what my new life will be. The Army is the only job I've ever done. I'll miss it. But I like a challenge too." Reading about Doughty's positive attitude in a USA Today article, Little Caesars founder Mike Ilitch offered him an opportunity to own his own franchise. "Even better than getting your own franchise is being an inspiration for their veterans program," said Doughty. In 2010 Ilitch won an award for his Wounded Veterans program from the US Department of Veterans Affairs.[17]

Kansas

"We cross the prairies as of old, the Pilgrims crossed the sea,
To make the West, as they the East, the homestead of the free."

-The Son of the Kansas Emigrant   John Greenleaf Whittier

Getting Out of Dodge

By late afternoon we arrived in St Louis and stopped at the arch. It was my first view of the landmark and I never knew it was possible to ride to the top. The ride is somewhere between the angled elevator ride of the Eiffel Tower and an enclosed Ferris wheel. The tiny rounded capsules only carry 5 people and the slanted windows of the arch walkway offer a dizzying view of the river and the city below. Due to the rain, I decided to paint in Missouri on the way back and we pushed west into Kansas. We stopped in Colby at a little campground just off the interstate next to the Prairie Museum, "home of the world's largest barn." Bourquin's campground also had a wonderful little restaurant where we enjoyed a steak dinner and the best bread pudding I have ever had. We took along a loaf of homemade bread for the journey. The evening brought thunderstorm warnings and in the morning I painted a sunrise picture of a little barn & horse corral. We took a side trip to Dodge City. The gunslinger shows may be a little cheesy, but the museum is a little treasure full of history.

H.L. Sitler, the first settler of what became Dodge City, said; "If you stood on the hill above Dodge City, there was traffic as far as you could see, 24-hours a day, seven days a week on the Santa Fe Trail."

Fort Dodge was one of the most important forts on the frontier, its primary purpose being to protect wagon trains from Indian attacks. Established in 1865, the men stationed there were often displaced Confederates, preferring fighting Indians to northern prisons. With no materials, their housing was sod dugouts on the banks of the Arkansas River. Earthen banks were bunks and a hole in the roof admitted light and air. By 1868, stone buildings replaced the huts and George Custer was the General.

SSgt Daniel Gilyeat was born in Shawnee Mission. He is of American Indian heritage with Pawnee and Delaware ancestry. Dan and his two brothers were raised by a single mother and rarely had running water and electricity; he obtained a high school diploma at an Indian Training School in Ronan, Montana in 1990. He re-enlisted in the Marines after the 9/11 attacks and deployed to Iraq on his first combat tour of duty in 2003. Returning to Iraq for his second tour of duty in 2005, he was wounded when the Humvee he was riding in was hit by a massive roadside bomb. The blast severed Sgt Gilyeat's left leg above the knee; he retained his composure and the control of the men he was responsible for by telling jokes. While a tourniquet was placed on his injured leg, Sgt Gilyeat told jokes until the medical team arrived. He walked on his prosthetic leg only 27 days after surgery, then ran for Congress in 2010.[18]

Nebraska

"My first years were spent living just as my forefathers had lived - roaming the green, rolling hills of what are now the states of South Dakota and Nebraska."

Standing Bear

Not in Kansas Anymore

I dropped Roger off in Denver so he could go camping with his daughter while I went to Nebraska and the Dakotas. I headed northeast towards Nebraska, trying to get north of an approaching storm system. Unfortunately I was little late. As I headed up two lane Route 71 with 50 miles to the Nebraska border, the RV's weather band began issuing warnings of tornados, 2 inch hail and up to 70 mph gusts. Of course they issued them by county and I had no idea what county I was in. (Ignorance is not always bliss – sometimes it is just ignorance.) I began to panic as I passed one of the county signs they had just announced. I got in line behind 2 horse trailers also fleeing north, figuring that I could follow them if they turned in at a farm. There was nowhere to turn an RV around, the sky ahead was black and the strengthening storm was headed south. Tornado scenarios began to play out as I envisioned having to ditch the RV, find a culvert and hang onto a cat 'and my little dog, too.' As I crossed the border into Nebraska, the sky finally began to lighten. I pulled over and breathed at the I-80 intersection.

Forecasts to the north were warmer so I moved on to Gering for the evening. I had a beautiful view of Scotts Bluff National Monument and Mitchell Pass from my campsite and a glowing sunset to end a day of intensity. In the morning, I painted the monument under cloudy skies. Called the "Gibraltar of Nebraska", Mitchell Pass was a significant progress marker for settlers on the Oregon Trail. At the Monument's Oregon Trail Museum, they have the largest art collection of William Henry Jackson. Hired as a bullwhacker for a Montana freighting outfit, Jackson photographed and painted the west. His photographs of Yellowstone were used to convince Congress to establish the first National Park in 1872. Most of his work was completed in his 90's.

National Guard Sgt. Jenny Beck Bos, Columbus, (shown with part of her company) is one of many "citizen soldiers"; a grade school teacher, mother and the first woman in Nebraska history to win a bronze star for valor in combat. During a fierce insurgent ambush, Bos was driving an armored truck and stopped to rescue her fellow soldiers, pulling a 205 pound trapped and wounded comrade from his wrecked vehicle and out of the line of fire. She donated her uniform and relics to the Nebraska History Museum.[19]

South Dakota

"I see a time of Seven Generations
when all the colors of mankind will
gather under the Sacred Tree of Life
and the whole Earth will become one
circle again."
  ~ Tashunka Witko   'Crazy Horse'

Mountain Men

The weather was beautiful in South Dakota and I spent the evening in Angostura State Park, just south of the Black Hills and Mount Rushmore, and painted the lake view the following morning before heading north. The RV restrictions prevented me from taking the scenic tunnel approach to Rushmore – I was one inch too wide – but I was no less impressed by my first look at the monument. Photos do not do it justice. I walked the trail that takes you closer to the faces and past the sculptor Gutzon Borglum's studio. One of the original carvers was at the ranger presentation showing the small tools used for the carving.

In 1939, while Borglum was already blasting and carving, sculptor Korczak Ziolkowski was getting a letter from Standing Bear asking him to sculpt the Crazy Horse Memorial. Crazy Horse is a beloved hero because he was unflinching in his beliefs. He upheld tribal teachings, refused to sell tribal lands or be moved onto reservations. He was known as a man of peace, but when forced to defend his tribe's sovereignty, he was a leader in battle and willing to die for his beliefs.

Ziolkowski would have to wait until after his own battles in World War II to start the carving. One of the reasons the monument remains unfinished after more than 60 years of work is that Ziolkowski refused all government funding. Only donations and admission fees to view the ongoing work are used to pay for it. Ziolkowski died in 1982 and is buried in a tomb at the foot of the Crazy Horse Monument and Thunderhead Mountain. He took no pay and worked in obscurity, often completely alone. His wife and seven of their children carry on the project.

As a young Army sergeant in Viet Nam in 1969, Gene Murphy of Sioux Falls was paralyzed by two gunshots to his right side. Mr. Murphy's long history of advocacy on behalf of disabled veterans began almost immediately on his return from Vietnam. He has served for 20 years on the South Dakota Veterans Commission. He served as *DAV* National Commander in 1987-88. Mr. Murphy was named South Dakota's Handicapped Citizen of the Year in 1979.[20]

North Dakota

"Where they call it the Red River Valley of the North, there are no mountains,
The floor is wide as a glacial lake—Agassiz, the fields go steady to the horizon,
Sunflower, potato, summer fallow, corn, and so flat that a shallow ditch
Can make tractor drivers think of Columbus and the edge."
-Early Cutting   Roland Flint

Little sod house on the prairie

In the morning I headed north through Newell, the sheep capitol of the US. The landscape was flat with bluffs and a few small volcanic hills. It was a beautiful warm day as I passed fields of sheep and sunflowers. I did a double take at one large herd of sheep – and had to take a picture of the burro standing in the middle of the flock. Later I learned that burros are used as guards against predators such as coyotes. As I crossed the border into North Dakota, I looked for a place to paint, deciding to go to Bowman to see what a small town had to offer. At a tourist information station, a young woman directed me to a sod house and old church behind the museum. I put my awning out for shade and included the John Deere tractor in the painting.

The Homestead Act was signed by Abraham Lincoln in 1862. Any man or woman twenty-one years old or the head of a family could have 160 acres of undeveloped land by living on it five years and paying eighteen dollars in fees. They were also required to build a home, make improvements and farm the land before they could own it outright. As an alternative, they could purchase the land for $1.25 per acre after having lived on the land for six months.

The prairie lacked standard building materials such as wood or stone; however, sod from thickly-rooted prairie grass was abundant. Construction of a sod house involved cutting patches of sod in rectangles and piling them into walls. They could accommodate normal doors and windows and a variety of roofing materials, including sod roofs. The resulting home was well-insulated and inexpensive, if somewhat damp and prone to insects. Stucco or wood panels often protected the outer walls and canvas or plaster often lined the interior walls. Many decades later, the sod-house architecture was given credit for being one of the main factors making the United States the greatest agricultural nation in the world.

Sgt. Sam Floberg of Fargo lost part of his right leg in a 2006 rocket-propelled grenade attack in Afghanistan. Although Floberg's injuries from a deadly attack are evident, his sense of humor puts people at ease. ND Veterans Affairs Commissioner Lonnie Wangen nominated the NDSU business student for the American Patriot Award "… Sam's attitude has inspired these Soldiers (who served with him) and I still hear them speak of what an inspiration Sam is today." *The American Patriot Program* is made up of 9 baseball organizations from across the country that are "united to honor the combat wounded Veteran through America's national pastime."[21]

Wyoming

"I saw the hawk ride updraft in the sunset over Wyoming.

It rose from coniferous darkness, past gray jags

Of mercilessness, past whiteness, into the gloaming

Of dream-spectral light above the lazy purity of snow-snags."

- Mortal Limit   Robert Penn Warren

'The Register of the Desert'

As I arrived at camp in Devil's Tower in Wyoming my low fuel light came on. But the late afternoon light on the monument was brilliant so I ignored the warning and drove up to the trail anyway. The most impressive thing about the tower's formation is the shape and size of the columns. Massive pieces that have broken off during the formation litter the trail and the resulting tower is made up of hexagonal columns which remained due to the hexagon's structural strength. At sunset I noticed I was alone on the trail and, seeing the 'bear country' signs, I quickly went back to camp.

Two days later, after meeting Roger, we left camp at Pathfinder Dam on Route 220 and passed Independence Rock, another milestone on the Oregon Trail. It was named because a fur trapper leading the first wagon train arrived there on July 4th. They inscribed their names on the rock and began a tradition of still readable inscriptions left by many of the 550,000 settlers who traveled the Oregon Trail. It was nicknamed the "Register of the Desert." Reading the inscriptions, I reflected on my decision the previous day to drive to Devil's Tower on an empty tank. Such carefree choices would have been deadly decisions for the settlers. Continuing west to the Tetons I met a friend of mine who was there painting. We walked to Colter Bay to try to capture the light on the peaks. The following day we detoured to Jackson for an RV repair. Our dog became a tourist celebrity by pointing a stuffed bison outside a store in downtown Jackson. The following day it was on to Yellowstone where we spent several days and my favorite part of the trip. I will simply say in this small space that to go to Yellowstone is to pause and watch the planet breathe.

Lt. Lee Alley (Ret.), Wheatland, is a Vietnam veteran who, at 21, earned the Distinguished Service Cross and two Purple Hearts. Four Star General Tommy Franks (then a 1st Lt.) served alongside Lee in 1967- 68. He said "Lee is a true patriot and a bona-file American Hero. He led his troops with honor and distinction…" When he came home, Alley was berated on college campuses and never spoke of his military experience. Thirty two years later, he wrote a book to help heal the returning servicemen from Iraq and Afghanistan. "Back from War" is a guide to readjustment to civilian life drawing on his own and 12 other contributors' experiences. "Anyone spouting the demise of our American youth's patriotism... never had the honor of commanding those like I did in combat."[22]

Montana

"Eventually, all things merge into one...and a river runs through it."
-A River Runs Through It

Norman MacLean

Trails, Trapping and Trading

We crossed the state line just outside the Yellowstone exit and headed toward Bozeman, then on to Helena for the night. The scenic road north took us through Choteau, entering the Blackfoot reservation at Browning. With all our political correctness, we could not help but laugh at the reservation's high school mascot sign: "Home of the Indians"

It was a short drive to East Glacier and the Glacier National Park entrance. We stopped to pick up a rental car since the road through the park is not open to RVs. The park is magnificent, the moist greens and wildflowers against the blue of the enormous mountains and sky. The approaching storm clouds to the northwest added to the drama of the scenery and we were lucky to almost complete the road before the rain finally came. The next day we headed west on Route 2 before the severe weather moved in. In Kalispell I painted a quick sketch of the river.

For 10,000 years the human inhabitants of the Glacier region were Native Americans who hunted and trapped. The first Europeans came for the same reasons, soon followed by the miners and settlers. Southeast of Glacier, Fort Benton, called the 'birthplace of Montana', was built by the American Fur Company. When the Blackfeet requested that the company move their post at Fort Lewis across the Missouri River, they complied. The new Fort Benton was built of adobe for warmth and had a small door which allowed the Blackfoot traders in a few at a time to trade their pelts. By the time the fur trade died in 1865, the future of Montana was established. The Blackfoot trade made relations with the tribe safe for settlers, the trails they blazed were mapped for the new inhabitants and the wealth from the fur trade built the new Territory.

Capt. Eivind Forseth was a second lieutenant with the 82nd Airborne Division when his convoy was hit by an IED in January 2005 in Mosul. His shattered arm would require 30 surgeries and thousands of hours of rehabilitation. He was initially hesitant to try a new fly fishing program at Walter Reed Hospital. He grew up fly fishing the big waters in central Montana before enlisting in the U.S. Army. With the encouragement of his mother and the Chief of Occupational Therapy, he gave it a try. "The first day out, I hooked a Rainbow. It saved my life." As a Captain he became instrumental in getting *Project Healing Waters* established and eventually became one of the Board of Directors of the program after his retirement.[23]

Idaho

"A beautiful open plain, partially supplied with pine, now presented itself."

-Lewis & Clark Journal

Submarines in the Mountains

It was a scenic drive across Route 2 from Montana to Idaho. We came into the beautiful town of Bonners Ferry as some rain clouds threatened from the northwest.

We continued down Route 2 and found many great painting sites dotted with beautiful old barns and farms but unfortunately no place to pull over the RV. Eventually I found a sunlit field of hay bales to paint while Roger went for a run. Although I was seeing relatively little of Idaho, I had heard that this was an especially scenic part. The rain let up as we headed south and stopped for the night at Farragut State Park on Lake Pend Oreille.

Named for Admiral David Farragut who was the leading Naval officer of the Civil War, the lake was originally spotted from the air by Eleanor Roosevelt on a flight to Seattle. Following Pearl Harbor, President Roosevelt was searching for a protected naval training site. He made a secret visit to the site, ground was broken in March 1942, and by September the base had a population of 55,000, making it the largest city in Idaho. It became the second largest naval training station in the world. Over 293,000 sailors received basic training at Farragut during its 30 months of existence. The last recruit graduated in March 1945 and the facility was decommissioned in June 1946. It was also used as a POW camp where nearly 900 Germans worked as gardeners and maintenance men. Closed to the public, a Naval submarine research base still operates on the Lake and there is the occasional strange sight of a submarine surfacing on the mountain lake.

Andrew Pike, Twin Falls, was on a foot patrol with the 82nd Airborne near Tikrit on March 26, 2007, just 30 meters from his compound, when he was paralyzed from the waist down by a sniper's bullet. *Canine Companions for Independence* paired him with with Yazmin, a black lab assistance dog, funded by Crane Aerospace in Redmond, WA. It's easy to see why Yazmin is important to Pike. "When Yazmin pulls my wheelchair my hands are free to carry my daughter on my lap," he said. Pike is pursuing a spot on the Paralympics archery team, taking college courses and considering a future as a Physician's Assistant. About his disability he said, "It won't stop me from doing anything I want to do."[24]

Washington

"Our bare feet are conscious of the sympathetic touch, for the soil is rich with the life of our kindred."

Chief Seattle

-As recorded by Dr. Henry A. Smith. There is no known accurate record of Chief Seattle's 1854 speech. Smith's 1887 article is the only written account which he is said to have translated from the Chief's native language.

Volcanoes, Apple Seeds and the Great Spirit

We picked up Route 821 through the Yakima Valley, a road recommended by an Oregon painter friend. It was a beautiful river and I snapped pictures all along the way. Along Route 12 to Mt. Rainier, I found some late afternoon light on an old red apple truck and jumped out to paint. With no light left we found a national forest campsite and did our best to level the RV. The next morning under clouds closing in, we caught a partial glimpse of majestic Mt Rainier, the highest point in Washington.

At the Rainier ranger station we got some information on Mt. St Helens which was just to the south. According to Indian legend, Mt. St Helens was a sacred place, the symbol of a fiery woman (Loo-wit) in a love triangle with the two sons. The Great Spirit changed the woman into Mt. St Helens and the two sons into Mt. Adams and Mt. Hood. On the ranger's advice, we took I-5 and route 504 to the Visitor Center closest to the crater. It was well worth the trip. Just seeing the remaining crater, the dead trees, stumps and massive lava fields attested to the scope and power of the 1980 eruption. The wall of rocks and ash had hit with speeds up to 670 mph.

During the previous eruption period in the 1840's, the apple seed had recently arrived in Washington and was found to be especially suited to the volcanic soil. Josiah Red Wolf planted the first seeds near the Snake River. The lives of an Iowa family who were traveling to the west coast carting 700 grafted fruit trees were saved by their cargo. According to daughter Eliza Lewelling's account of her father's good fortune, "the Indians believed that the Great Spirit lived in trees; they thought that he must be under the special care of the Great Spirit, and so they did not harm him."

Billy Foster, Bremerton, is a wounded veteran who served 14 years in the Army. His tours of duty included two deployments to Bosnia, one to Saudi Arabia and one to Iraq. Foster suffered a traumatic brain injury and has worked through these difficulties to become a strong leader and contributor on the *Skookum* Wheeled Vehicle contract at Fort Lewis. He also is a single father and hero to his daughter. Being a part of the familiar military culture at Fort Lewis Vehicle Maintenance, Foster is a positive influence on the young men and women as they come and go from the war torn countries of Iraq and Afghanistan.[25]

Oregon

"There will be plenty of time now, time that will smell of fires,
And drying leather, and catalogues, and apple cores.
The farmers clean their boots, and whittle, and drowse."

Oregon Winter   Jeanne McGahey

Formerly Known as Mazama

Heading down I-5 through Portland, we got as far as Woodburn by dark, so we were happy to have one of those parking lot type RV parks conveniently facing the interstate.

It was wonderful to take a break from the road for a day and I went painting with a friend from Eugene. We found a horse pasture near Fall Creek to do a quick painting. The problem with painting horses is that as soon as you set up, they all come over to the fence right in front of you.

The following day it was back on the road to head to Crater Lake. At this point, I was becoming concerned with how much grandeur my brain could hold. We spent the afternoon on the perimeter of the crater and took the long hike down to the boat launch. The water is cold, amazingly blue and a few kids take a dip just to say they did. I was content with observing.

Crater Lake was formed by the eruption of Mt. Mazama about 7700 years ago. Archaeologists have found Indian artifacts buried under the ash from that eruption. The Klamath Indians, descendants of the Makalaks, still regard the lake as sacred. In their legend two holy men jumped into the volcano to quell its fire. When the sun rose, the volcano had been replaced by a lake. It was believed that to look upon the surface resulted in death.

For this reason, the early settlers did not hear about the lake or its location from the natives. It was happened upon by the settlers when they began to search for gold in the 1850's. It was not named Crater Lake until a boat was lowered to the lake and explored the cinder cone on Wizard Island. It is the deepest lake in the country at nearly 2000 feet.

Army Cpl. Nick Edinger, Central Point, lost his left foot to an improvised explosive device in Afghanistan in March 2010. Edinger set off the mine because he was carrying extra equipment for a teammate with a back injury. While recuperating at Walter Reed Hospital, he participated in Soldier Ride, a 100 mile biking event of the *Wounded Warrior Foundation*. Edinger plans to go into the medical field after he recovers, refusing to let his disability beat him. "I'm not going to let that happen. Never. I've got a life to live." [26]

California

"And he says that the mountains are fairer
  For once being held in your thought;
That each rock holds a wealth that is rarer
  Than ever by gold-seeker sought"

-Truthful James' Answer to 'Her Letter'   Bret Harte

Red and Gold

It is estimated that 95% of the old growth redwoods have been cut. Of the remaining groves, about 50% are in the coastal region of southern Oregon and northern California. The Yurok tribe which dates back to the region 7000 years, used the easily split wood for houses and boats. The first European exploring the region was Jedediah Smith in 1829. A hunter and trapper, "Old Jed" is responsible for mapping much of the coastal region in advance of the gold rush.

California had just been ceded from Mexico at the time of the gold rush. Of over 300,000 who came to stake their claim, tens of thousands came by ship from Latin America, Europe, Australia, and China. The port of San Francisco became a boom town and California was rushed to statehood by 1850. When the rush ended, many miners turned to logging the giant redwoods for a living, which forced the Yurok and other tribes onto reservations. Local and state organizations fought to protect the forests beginning in 1918, but it was not until 1968 that Redwoods National Park was established.

At Jedediah Smith Park just over the Oregon border, we took a short hike through a grove of the giant trees, in awe of their mammoth size and the quiet world under the canopy. They do not lend themselves to small paintings, so we went south to Crescent City and coastal highway 101. I stopped to paint a beautiful scene at the edge of the redwoods overlooking the rocks at Two Sisters. Then for the first time in weeks, we headed east. Route 299 to Redding winds through the coastal range with breathtaking views of Mt. Shasta to the north and we followed it east to the Lassen Volcano.

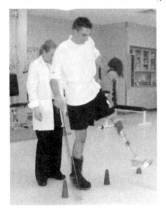

Navy Corpsman Derek McGinnis, Freemont, was part of a medical team serving the Marines in Iraq when a he was hit by a car bomb. It severed his left leg above the knee and he suffered eye and brain injuries. When he woke up he couldn't speak or eat. After a year of surgeries, and physical and speech therapy, he was outfitted with a prosthetic leg. When he was released from the hospital in November 2005, he vowed to run a 10K race. Now McGinnis bicycles, surfs and swims, and trains for several biathlons a year. "My job now is to be a good civilian and raise my boys to be honorable men" said McGinnis. He wrote *Exit Wounds* as a guide to pain management and is an *Amputee Outreach Advocate*.[27]

Nevada

"The saddest day hath gleams of light, The darkest wave hath bright foam beneath it,
There twinkles o'er the cloudiest night, Some solitary star to cheer it."   Sarah Winnemucca

"In Nevada, for a time, the lawyer, the editor, the banker, the chief desperado, the chief gambler,
and the saloon-keeper occupied the same level of society, and it was the highest."

-Roughing It

Mark Twain

Luck, a Pink Beetle and the Pony Express

There is much more to Nevada than Vegas but my painting subject seemed to be all about luck. If I had one of those GPS navigators people keep telling me I need, I would not have taken the I-80 Sparks exit and consequently would not have noticed I had a flat in one of my dual rear tires. Two blocks away we found a garage and I suddenly had two hours to kill in a new state. In a nearby alley, I found a sunlit pink vintage VW Beetle that made a perfectly fine painting subject. After a short time, the RV was ready and I had a little 6 x 8 painting. But as I would soon learn, it took a lot more than luck to get that VW on the road to Sparks, NV. Route 50 is called the "loneliest road in America" and it snakes across the state like a thread holding the past to the present. In parts the geography is so barren you can see an hour or more of the road ahead. Much of it follows stagecoach and Pony Express routes and stations, with historic markers to tell the tale. This ad from 1859 says it all:

> **WANTED**
> YOUNG SKINNY WIRY FELLOWS
> Not over eighteen. Must be expert riders willing to risk death daily. Orphans preferred. WAGES $25 per week. Apply Central Overland Express

Being an expert rider helped but markers indicated that being lucky was better. It was a brutal land for the riders, the settlers as well as the native tribes they fought. I was in awe of the people who settled there, endured the elements and dangers as I was in respect of the original owners of the land.

After the Pony Express came the telegraph and then the roads. Rt. 50 was then part of the Lincoln Highway, the first coast to coast road from New York to California, less than 50 years after the Pony Express. Moving troops along that road was a young Army Lieutenant Dwight Eisenhower who would promote the Interstate highway system when he became President. Luck? If World War II had ended differently, who knows if I-80 would have been built or what that VW would have looked like.

Craig Fitzgerald, Las Vegas, considers himself lucky. In his eighth year of military service, multiple gunshot wounds in an insurgent attack in Afghanistan in 2003 severely injured him. Eleven surgeries limited his arm movements but not his determination. After two years of rehabilitation, he and another veteran decided to hike the 2,200-mile Appalachian Trail, his "*Trail to Recovery*" project raising $150,000 to benefit wounded veterans and their families. [28]

Utah

"The sun of a late July burns varnish onto summit rock.
Wagons and teams go by. Escarpments for a moment block the scalding sky."
-To Utah

Edward L Hart

A Geologic Layer Cake with Fruit

Entering Utah, we finally left the Loneliest Road at Delta. By the time we got to Panguitch, it was dark and we turned in early so we could get to Bryce Canyon before sunrise. At Sunrise Point a large, but very hushed crowd gathered as the sky lightened. After the sun flooded the canyon with light, we walked down the trail through the giant formations. We decided to find a campsite to stay an extra day and used our bikes to ride down to Swamp Canyon where I painted a less intimidating Bryce landscape. At night we went to the visitor center where they had telescopes set up to view Jupiter's moons in the clear black sky.

Leaving Bryce the next day, we rode up Route 12 to Capitol Reef National Park. We have seen a lot of scenic roads on this trip but this had to be the winner for vastness. Unlike the reds and oranges of Bryce, Capitol Reef has more varied and subtle colors. The 10,000 feet of sedimentary strata found in Capitol Reef range in age from Permian (270 million years) to Cretaceous (80 million years). The Waterpocket Fold formed in the last 20 million years has tilted this geologic layer cake down to the east. Along Route 24, there is a museum and schoolhouse, the remnants of an old settlement.

Fruita was established by Mormons in 1880 at the junction of the Fremont River and Sulphur Creek. It became an important settlement due to its long growing season and abundant water. The settlers grew their own food, and were known for their fruit orchards. They set up a barter society which spared them when the great depression hit the rest of the country. The naming of Capitol Reef as a National Monument was the death knell for the community, bringing increased traffic and the eventual seizing of the land by the government. The orchards are still a noticeable part of the landscape and are still producing.

In 2005 a roadside bomb in Iraq hurled Bryant Jacobs from his Humvee. He required multiple surgeries and extensive rehab and there is still a possibility he may lose his left leg. "We'll see what happens" said Jacobs. He struggles with his balance and is in constant pain but has few complaints. The Riverton resident was recently given a specially adapted home from *Homes for Our Troops* and is giving back. A student at the University of Utah, he hosted a Charity Golf Tournament to raise money for another veteran's house. HFOT Founder John Gonsalves says Jacobs' commitment is typical of the veterans looking out for each other.[29]

Colorado

"Colorado men are we,
From the peaks gigantic, from the great sierras and the plateaus,
From the mine and from the gully, from the hunting trail we come,
Pioneers! O Pioneers!"
-Pioneers! O Pioneers

Walt Whitman

The Camelot of the High Plains

The painting was done on a previous trip to the Rist Canyon area northwest of Boulder. My unfinished business in Colorado was to see Rocky Mountain National Park. Going up Route 131 toward Topongas, we looked for a state park camp we had in our guide. Once we saw the two small ruts heading down into a forest, it was nearly dark. We decided to move on to an RV campground rather than risk getting stuck in a field. We got an early start the next morning to Trail Ridge Road and were lucky to have an absolutely perfect day with bright clear blue skies and puffy clouds. At the top, the air was cold and thin and we warmed up with some hot chocolate in the RV. We had our picture taken by another hiker at 12,000 feet then continued down the trail to the meadows below. There we found an elk herd and a very active bull courting his pick of the females right next to the road, quite oblivious to all the onlookers. Our trip back across the Rockies brought us once again to the plains. The Mountain Route of the Santa Fe Trail followed present day Route 50 from Kansas southwest through Colorado at Raton Pass to New Mexico. Though 100 miles further than the Cimarron Cutoff, the mountain trail was less prone to Indian attacks and had better water supplies.

Bent's Fort, built by fur traders William and Charles Bent in 1833, was a trading post and supply point. The fort welcomed all people along the Santa Fe Trail, including Indians, US soldiers, Mexicans, Germans, French, Irish and Blacks. It was a neutral place of refuge and safety. Free trade and talk and even inter-marriage were welcome at the fort. William Bent himself was married to a Cheyenne, named Owl Woman. The U.S. government failed to compensate Bent for housing and supplying Mexican and Indian War troops which began overrunning the fort. Finally a cholera epidemic decimated the plains tribes. Bent is believed to have partially burned and exploded the fort himself in frustration at the turn of events. Today, Bent's Old Fort has been reconstructed as a national historic site.

Marine Staff Sgt John Jones (Ret) of Fort Collins was severely injured in Operation Iraqi Freedom, in 2004, losing both legs below the knees. After 30 surgeries and rehabilitation he returned to active duty as an Operations and Training NCO in San Antonio, and also trained wounded veterans in marksmanship. After retiring, in 2008 he was chosen by the Wall Street Warfighters Foundation as one of the first candidates for their Financial Career Training Program for wounded veterans. He is also a national spokesman for the Wounded Warrior Disabled Sports Project[30]

Oklahoma

"Something called 'the Oklahoma Standard' became known throughout the world. It means resilience in the face of adversity. It means a strength and compassion that will not be defeated."

Governor Brad Henry

White Hair and Black Gold

My first trip through Oklahoma was plagued by tornado warnings, so I was glad for a second chance and fair weather to explore some back roads. Having met a lovely couple from Oklahoma the previous year when I did a painting of their horses out in New Mexico, I had in mind finding a nice horse farm to paint. We drove east to Bartlesville, the home of the Price Tower, Frank Lloyd Wright's only high rise and a very unique structure. Along the way on Route 60, I kept a lookout for horses. Passing through Pawhuska, I spotted a side road that looked promising for painting and found a great little barn and horse trailer. Asking permission to paint on their property, I was greeted with an invitation to set up anywhere I liked. Their teenage daughter watched my process intently as we chatted about her high school plans and the local area. I learned that I was not in horse country, but oil country.

Pawhuska was named for a famous Osage chief, Pahu-cka, or White Hair, who received his name from an incident in his youth. Wounding an officer wearing a powdered wig, he started to scalp his quarry when the whole scalp came off and the victim escaped. The warrior was left grasping a fluffy white wig in his hand!

Pawhuska is capital of the Osage Nation, the Native American owners of the county's mineral rights. Those rights made them the richest people per capita in the world during the 1920's oil boom. That fortune also made its way 20 minutes down the road to Bartlesville where H C Price started a petroleum company that would one day commission Wright's high rise.

Major Ed Pulido of Oklahoma City says he did not 'lose' anything when an Iraqi roadside bomb resulted in the amputation of his left leg. "I 'sacrificed' my leg defending my country. And I would do it again." Pulido serves with the *Folds of Honor Foundation* and *Vets for Victory* and has been a peer counselor at Brooke Army Medical Center on behalf of the Amputee Coalition of America. [31]

Missouri

My American image is made up of what I have come across, of what was 'there' in the time of my experience- no more, no less."

-Harry S Truman Library Interview   Thomas Hart Benton

Santa Fe or Bust

Continuing on Route 60 eastward through Springfield, we traveled across southern Missouri to find a place to paint. The once rural road was in the process of becoming a divided highway and was not what I expected. Just west of Poplar Bluff, I saw a road and barn as we were coming out of the hill country. The town of Fluechville (pronounced Flukeville) was appropriately the site of my painting. But it was no fluke how Missouri came to prominence in the westward expansion of the United States.

Following the Louisiana Purchase in 1803, President Jefferson commissioned the Lewis and Clark expedition to explore the Missouri River west of the Mississippi. On our westward trip through Missouri, we had followed Interstate 70 which parallels the important overland trails which made Missouri "the Gateway to the West." Boone's Lick Road, from St Charles to Franklin, was a trace forged by Indians and trappers before Daniel Boone explored it in the early 1800's and gave it a name. It eventually became the beginning of the Santa Fe, Salt Lake and Oregon Trails. A Virginia trader then settled near the town of Boone's Lick after the War of 1812. Heavily in debt from his business dealings, William Becknell decided to lead an expedition westward to the Rockies. His timing proved fortunate when his party ran into Mexican soldiers in Colorado who told him of the recent overthrow of Spanish rule. Santa Fe was hungry for trade and Becknell was the first to arrive, disposing of his goods at a profit. Returning to Missouri, he was able to pay off all his debts and organize a new expedition using the Cimarron cutoff through Oklahoma. Despite little water and exposure to Indian attacks, the non-mountainous route became the preferred route to the southwest and earned Becknell the title "Father of the Santa Fe Trail."

In 2004, Phillip Sturgeon, of Benton was stationed near Baghdad as a medic with the 458th Engineer Battalion when a rocket-propelled grenade struck the vehicle he was in. Four of Sturgeon's patrol were killed in the blast, and he suffered broken ribs, facial fractures, serious knee and shoulder injuries and brain trauma. After recovering, he was awarded a Mission Continues Fellowship to become a puppy trainer for *Support Dogs Inc.* of St. Louis, an organization that provides highly trained dogs to the disabled at no cost. Sturgeon said his goal is to open a training school near his home where in an effort to increase the number of support dogs that can be made available to those in need.[32]

Ohio

"All the armies of Europe, Asia and Africa combined, with all the treasure of the earth in their military chest; with a Bonaparte for a commander, could not by force, take a drink from the Ohio"

~ Abraham Lincoln

Africa, Ohio

With cold weather approaching, I decided to fly to Indianapolis to complete the seven Midwestern states I had not yet painted. It is a part of the country I am familiar with, having lived in Wisconsin for several years. Rain was in the forecast, so I followed the clear skies to Ohio. I went north through the farmlands to Van Wert and found the late afternoon sun and the first of many barns I would paint in the Midwest. Snapping pictures as I went north, I suddenly realized that I was close to nowhere with no hotel for the night. The nearest town of any size was Fayette just north of I-80. At a gas station, I was directed to a pizzeria whose owners also ran a bed and breakfast. I ordered a pizza and waited for the owner's wife, Jane who ran the B&B to return from the local

opera house. My first thought was that I was impressed that there was an opera house in a town without a motel. The Red Brick Inn was a very charming place and a great bargain, including Jane's home cooked French toast in the morning. We had a nice chat and she was very happy to see my painting from the previous day.

In the 50 years following its 1803 statehood, Ohio went from frontier to a diverse agricultural economy. Its population grew from 50,000 to over 2 million and it became a leader in the abolition of slavery. The most extensive Underground Railroad network in the country with at least 23 stations and 3000 miles of routes is estimated to have helped 40,000 pass through the state. Southeast of my painting site was the town of Africa, so named when it became an important station in the Underground Railroad. Samuel Patterson used his mansion as that station and helped build the Wesleyan Methodist Church. Many escaped slaves settled in the town, risking a return to slavery or much worse in order to help those who followed.

Mark R. Mix, Warsaw, first enlisted in the military as a Navy Seabee in February of 2001. After two deployments and two different injuries, the Navy veteran was paralyzed from the waist down by a mortar blast in Baghdad in 2004. He'd never been on skis before finding himself in a wheelchair, and tried it out for the first time during the 2005 winter sports clinic run by vet *Chris Devlin Young* of New Hampshire. He set his sights on becoming a role model for his children and showing them that "being in a wheelchair doesn't stop you from anything."[33]

Michigan

"Some folks long to travel
To lands across the sea,
To flirt with Kings and
Queens and Counts
And other royalty,
But me, I never cared for
fame,
The joy for which I pine,
Is to float for days down the
Manistee
With a fishing pal of mine."

Fred Tomkins

Rest and Drink Plenty of Grape Juice

Driving north a short distance I crossed into Michigan. When I envisioned this trip, my plan was to go across the Upper Peninsula into Wisconsin. But my new traveling companion – a head cold – weakened my resolve. I began popping zinc tablets and eating French fries to avoid the inevitable stomach ache they caused. (So began my healthy travel diet). I decided to just find something to paint while it was still warm outside. Heading northwest I began to enter the rolling hills and vineyards of Van Buren County and after some treks down dirt roads, I found a good place to park and a little road next to some fall colored vineyards to paint. Finding that scene in southern Michigan was such a surprise and it added to my belief that America is full of wonderful secrets in every state that you can only find by unplanned travel.

To the north of my vineyard scene was the Van Buren county seat of Paw Paw, named for the native pawpaw trees which used to be abundant in the area. In addition to the fruit bearing pawpaw, the soil was found to be very suitable for grapes. Thomas Welch was a New Jersey dentist who was called upon to provide wine for the Wesleyan Methodists' communion. Since the church decried the use of alcohol, Welch decided to bottle "unfermented wine." While not an immediate success, the beginning of prohibition boosted public knowledge of the product and Welch was poised for the boom in sales and expanded their operation from New York to Michigan and adjoining states. The majority of the Michigan grapes are used for juices and jams and the vineyards are largely part of the National Grape Cooperative Association, the parent company of Welch Foods.

Troy Crawford of Lincoln Park deployed twice to Iraq, once in the Marine Corps and once in the Army. He was wounded by an improvised explosive device (IED) in 2006. As part of his recovery, he took up white water kayaking. He was awarded a full *Mission Continues* Fellowship volunteering at *Team River Runner* in Rockville, Maryland. He now helps other wounded service members learn to kayak as part of their recoveries.[34]

Wisconsin

"Through Wisconsin haze, I see the water gleam, the small craft tilt,
And through the clustering stems, the small waves lap upon the glacial silt"

-For John Muir, a Century and More after His Time   Janet Loxley Lewis

Brushes with Cheese

The rain arrived the following morning in Illinois, so I looked to adjoining states for clear skies. Just about the time I crossed the border into Wisconsin, the rain began falling in sheets. Wisconsin has beautiful and varied scenery from Door County in the northeast to the dells and bluffs in the west. The better forecast was to the west so I drove to La Crosse. The late afternoon sun came out over a nice farm and I set up only to discover my brushes were missing. By the time I went into town to buy a few brushes, it was cold and the light was gone. I was in a very foul mood, having lost about $300 worth of brushes, so I found a hotel for the night. The next day I looped back through Wisconsin from Iowa at Prairie du Chien. I painted an old hotel on the Mississippi, the refurbishing project of an older gentleman who envisioned tourists arriving in trains from Madison. The local man who told me the story doubted it would ever be finished. But I admired his dream and it reminded me of why I was on this trip. My little problems led me to places where I may not have painted otherwise. Wisconsin history is full of people carving out the farms that became "America's Dairy land." The early Wisconsin farmers grew wheat, a reliable crop requiring little investment, but one subject to soil depletion and insects. Commercial cheese making first began in 1837 and by the time Wisconsin became a state in 1848 dairy farming was practiced on a small scale for personal and community use. In 1866, N.W. Morley moved to Sauk County, Wisconsin from Ohio's dairy rich Lake County. Morley grew dissatisfied with growing wheat and bought as many head of dairy cows as he could. He began making butter and cheese, soon opening a factory. Others followed suit and by 1872, the area was completely transformed economically.

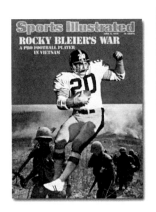

After his 1968 rookie season with the Pittsburgh Steelers, Rocky Bleier of Appleton was drafted into the U.S. Army. He shipped out to Vietnam in May 1969 and served with the 196th Light Infantry Brigade. While on patrol, Bleier was wounded in the left thigh when his platoon was ambushed. While he was down, a grenade landed nearby, sending shrapnel into his right leg. Upon his return, he couldn't walk without pain and weighed only 180 pounds. He spent two years trying to regain a spot on the Steelers active roster, and was waived on two occasions. But Bleier never gave up. At the time of his retirement in 1980, he was the Steelers fourth all-time leading rusher. He serves on the *Beating the Odds Foundation* Board.[35]

Minnesota

"This is America - a town of a few thousand, in a region of wheat and corn and dairies and little groves."

~ Main Street

Sinclair Lewis

Sacred Land in a Brutal Time

I have been to St Paul as well as northern Minnesota before, specifically on the shore of Lake Superior in winter for the only thing resembling mountain skiing you can do in the Midwest. I remember how bitterly cold Lutsen Mountain was and that it boasted an 800 ft vertical drop into a headwind off Lake Superior. Olympic medalist Cindy Nelson got her start there on what used to be her grandfather's land. In the southeastern part of the state, I got on scenic route 16 west of La Crescent and the sun was peeking through the clouds enough to light up a barn. I took advantage of the weather to do a quick painting.

The village of Hokah, named for Chief Wecheschatope Hokah was once an Indian village. The 1862 Dakota War was one of the saddest chapters in US history. The demands of the Civil War resulted in late payments and treaty violations by the US government, threatening the Dakota with starvation.

The resulting brutality from both sides against civilians pushed settlers from the land and pushed the Indians out of state to internment camps. It also resulted in the largest mass execution in US history when 38 Dakota warriors received the death penalty. Alfred Hill, an archaeologist who served in the infantry during the Dakota War became devoted to surveying the effigy mounds which dated back to 700 AD. The mounds, in the shapes of birds, mammals and fish, were being plowed under when the settlers returned to Minnesota after the war. Southeastern Minnesota was considered sacred land and the effigy mounds were believed to have been used in religious rituals and burials. Hill's field archaeologist, TH Lewis, surveyed 7000 mounds in Minnesota including the Hokah Mounds in 1884. Hill used his own fortune to fund the survey and his home in St. Paul was the center of the most extensive archaeological activity ever privately initiated and supported on the American continent. Very few of the Minnesota Mounds remain today.

Sergeant Neil Duncan from Maple Grove was severely injured in Afghanistan in December 2005 by an IED. Five days later, he woke up in the hospital missing both of his legs, breathing through a tube in his neck and could not talk. While undergoing rehabilitation at Walter Reed Army Medical Center, he became involved in Disabled Sports USA's and climbed Mt. Kilimanjaro in August, 2010. Duncan is an employee of the *Wounded Warrior Project.* "I know the sky is the limit for what can be accomplished."[36]

Iowa

"Once the land touches you, the wind never blows so cold again. You feel for it, like it was your child. When that happens to you, you can't be bought."

-Shoeless Joe'   W P Kinsella

Big River

With thick clouds overhead, I was drawn to an autumn orange colored field on a hillside in northeastern Iowa. Like Minnesota, Iowa is very rural and full of great barns, herds of horses and cattle and beautiful color. Similar effigy mounds to those mentioned in Minnesota are visible at Effigy Mounds National Monument in near Marquette. There are 206 mounds in the park, 31 of which are animal shaped. It is believed that tribal clans built the mounds and like most tribal nations, their fortunes changed over time.

Iowa means "the beautiful land" and its dominion was contested long before the first white men appeared in the state. Native people dated back more than 12,000 years and throughout their history tribes had to relinquish their land to more powerful tribes. Their territorial battles were no less brutal than those that would follow the arrival of Europeans. The name "Sioux" for the Dakota and Lakota tribes comes from the Algonquin word for "enemy" or "snake."

In 1673 French explorers Marquette and Joliet were the first white men to set foot in Iowa. Father Marquette was a beloved figure whose desire was to bring Christianity to the Indians, while Joliet wanted to find the Mississippi for trade. Their canoes spilled out from the Wisconsin River onto the Mississippi on June 17, in Marquette's words "with a joy which I cannot express." Near the southern border of Iowa, they followed an Indian path 6 miles west of the river. Recording a land rich with buffalo and fertile plains, they were greeted with peace pipes and a feast by an Illini tribe. Other explorers and traders would traverse Iowa before France sold it as part of the Louisiana Purchase. A series of treaties influenced by alcohol and gambling removed most of Iowa's native population. Of 16 tribes once in Iowa, only the Mesquakie remain today.

In August of 2003, the Humvee carrying B.J. Jackson and two other soldiers struck a land mine and was then hit by a rocket propelled grenade. Jackson lost both legs and suffered severe burns on his arms, legs and back. He spent nearly 50 days in the post burn unit. Remarkably, by early December, the Des Moines native was skiing on his new legs. One of five soldiers credited with inspiring the formation of *Building Homes for Heroes*, B.J. has made hundreds of television appearances and has been keynote speaker at numerous events.[37]

Illinois

"Know that the river has its destination. The elders say we must let go of the shore, push off into the middle of the river, keep our eyes open and our heads above the water. And I say see who is there with you and celebrate."

Hopi Elders

Draining the Swamp

I stayed in Geneseo in western Illinois and I would have liked to paint there. The rain clouds were moving from the west this time and I calculated a small window to paint in eastern Illinois if I got an early start. Just past dawn, I arrived in Kankakee - remembering the Arlo Guthrie song, 'City of New Orleans': "The train pulls out of Kankakee, rolls along past houses, farms and fields..." I picked out Kankakee River State Park on the state map by pure instinct and was relieved that it was a pretty wooded area with small bluffs by the river. The clouds were moving in, so I was happy to paint the light from the disappearing sun reflecting on the water. Following the Revolution, Illinois, Ohio, Indiana, Michigan and Wisconsin, were part of the Northwest Territory. In order to ratify the Articles of Confederation, four eastern states who had claims on the territory had to cede those claims to the federal government, making the land available for survey and sale. Illinois was rushed to statehood in 1818 even though its population was 24,000 below the statehood requirement at the time. A free state was needed to balance Mississippi and Alabama which had just been added as slave states. It was reported that population numbers were recounted several times until the requisite number was reached. The Potawatomi Indians called the Kankakee area 'Theatiki', which had several different meanings. One was 'wonderful land'. The Kankakee River was bordered with trees, rolling hills and bluffs and was abundant with wildlife. Another meaning was 'swampy place'. The part of the river plain that was swampland was drained and cultivated by the pioneers, chasing out horse thieves and criminals who took cover there. The first settlers moved to southern Illinois, preferring the wooded land to the prairie. By 1860, Chicago became the 9th largest city, holding the Republican Convention that nominated Abraham Lincoln.

Sgt. 1st Class Mike Schlitz of Moline, a 33-year-old Ranger-qualified soldier, was severely burned by an improvised explosive device in Baghdad in 2007. Schlitz received burns over 85 percent of his body, lost both hands and was left with a severely disfigured face. He spent over 10 months in the hospital and, 3 years in rehabilitation and has had over 56 surgeries. As part of Operation Proper Exit, SFC. Schlitz returned to Iraq building troop morale, mentoring, peer support and suicide prevention. [38]

Indiana

"Oh, the moonlight's fair tonight along the Wabash
  From the fields there comes a breath of new mown hay
Through the sycamores the candle lights are gleaming
  On the banks of the Wabash far away."

Paul Dresser

The Frontier Expands

In recent years I had become more familiar with Indiana when my husband, Roger, took me to Purdue University alumni weekends. Visiting West Lafayette I got an entirely different picture than on my previous quick trips on I-80. My more informed impression of Indiana was that it stood for everything honest and decent about America. If I were to describe what heartland means, it would be the people of Indiana. Crossing I-80 from Michigan, I headed down Routes 15 and 13 and immediately began to see Amish buggies and beautiful farmland. I knew my time was limited before the rainstorm that was predicted moved in. I quickly found an Amish barn near Millersburg and did a small painting just as the cold winds whipped up. Fifty years before the Amish could raise their barns, a small group had to fight the British for that right. George Rogers Clark was a Virginian who, getting financial support from Patrick Henry, set out to secure the Ohio River Valley from the British during the Revolution. The English Army was paying Native Americans to kill American settlers as punishment for disobeying their order not to settle west of the Appalachians. Clark raised a small army of 180 pioneer farmers and French volunteers to take on the British along the Ohio River. They had no military uniforms, only the animal skinned clothes they usually wore. The small army only had short-handled axes, Kentucky long rifles and knives - normal household equipment for the frontier. To reach Fort Vincennes, the men waded through shoulder high frozen floodwaters on the Little Wabash. To the north on the Wabash and near the town that would bear his name, French General Lafayette fought the British alongside the Americans in exchange for religious freedom for the French settlers. When the American Revolution ended in 1783, the United States gained all of the land between the Appalachian Mountains and the Mississippi.

Corporal Klay South knows a lot about sacrifice. The 30-year-old Marine, who grew up in Greenwood, chose to serve his country twice in Iraq, and was also twice wounded in battle. His second tour of duty in 2004 nearly took his life. Klay kicked open a door and was met by gunfire. His jaw and tongue were destroyed along with 22 of his teeth. But South didn't retreat. He has created a non-profit charity called *Veterans of Valor* to help wounded military service members.[39]

Delaware

"In the morning, the boardwalk opened, wide and white with sun, gulls on one leg in the slicks. Cold waves, cold air, and people out in heavy coats, arm in arm along the sheen of waves."
-A Few Lines from Rehoboth Beach   Fleda Brown

Beaches and Borders

I combined my final cluster of unfinished states with a family visit back to the northeast. I drove south from Philadelphia to Delaware with the idea of returning to a spot I had visited in high school. I skirted around Wilmington and Dover, passing up beautiful historic landmark buildings along the way before heading through farms and fields toward the eastern shore. In 1968, Lewes, Delaware was a quiet historic town I visited during an oceanography field trip. Lewes has grown considerably but still has its history intact. I stopped to snap some photos of the downtown before heading to the beach. It was late afternoon and I found a beautiful dune to paint before the last light of the day escaped.

In 1631, a Dutch expedition landed in Lewes after purchasing the land from local Indians. The tribe executed one of their members for stealing a coat of arms from the Dutch ship. Even though the Dutch did not want the man killed, the friends of the slain Indian wiped out the new colony in retaliation. Delaware was finally conveyed to the British and in 1662, King Charles II gave William Penn the land to the north of Delaware. The Duke of York, who controlled Delaware, ordered a 12 mile arc from the center of New Castle to form the arc on the present southern Pennsylvania border. He later tried to give Delaware to Penn. Lord Baltimore, who owned Maryland, argued that Delaware belonged to him. A committee in England decided that since Lewes and Cape Henlopen were already settled prior to Lord Baltimore, it belonged to Penn. They were to draw a line west from Cape Henlopen to a midpoint then straight north. But the coordinates were mistakenly drawn from Fenwick Island, nearly 30 miles to the south, resulting in the current borders. By 1776 Delaware declared itself free from Pennsylvania as well as England. It was the first state to ratify the Constitution.

Sgt. Jason Nielson of Milford was on patrol in October 2005 in Baghdad when a sniper's bullet pierced his spine. Like other severely wounded soldiers, Nielson returned home to many months of painful therapy and the prospect of life confined to a wheelchair. Nielson was aided in his recovery by *Operation First Response*, *Homes for Our Troops* and the *Paralyzed Veterans of America*, where he got the fraternal support he needed. He said "I am proud that I served my country. I would not change a thing even if the outcome was worse, even if I had a choice. Serving my country was easy to me, it felt natural. Learning to walk again at 27 was hard."[40]

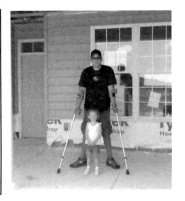

Maryland

"The clustered spires of Frederick stand
Green-walled by the hills of Maryland."
-Barbara Friethie

John Greenleaf Whittier

A Pig in a Pocomoke

The Delmarva Peninsula named after the 3 states it includes, is the thin strip of land between Chesapeake Bay and the Atlantic Ocean. It is comprised of small towns, state and national parks, seashores and tourist towns. The middle 50 miles of the eastern shore belongs to Maryland, a state of distinct regions. From the western mountains, through DC to the coastal plain, it is small but very diverse both in its geography and its people. On this trip I stopped in the small town of Snow Hill and the Pocomoke River where I found a water lily covered inlet to paint. I was greeted by small boats of fishermen who cruised down the river.

A 'poke' was the archaic word for 'bag' from the French word "pogue." The expression "Don't buy a pig in a poke" came from livestock carried to market in a sack. Buyers needed to examine the livestock before buying.

The town of Furnace Hill once stood 4 miles from Snow Hill in the Pocomoke Forest. The Furnace Town Museum now commemorates the iron ore industry and town it created. The Maryland Iron Company was created by the state government in 1828. They built a blast furnace in 1832 to smelt the area's bog iron ore into rounded metal "pigs."

The pig iron was sold to manufacturing industries near Philadelphia. Despite their high yield, they produced an inferior product and the property was auctioned to Thomas Spence for $3000 in 1837. This included every item in the town, corn fields, houses and even furniture. Misled about the quality of the bog ore, he invested all his (and his wife's) money in finding a better way to produce the metal. Furnace Hill boomed for 10 years until it faced labor shortages and poor market conditions. The production of iron ceased and Furnace Town became a ghost town. The forest reclaimed the land except for the brick blast furnace which still stands.

EMS Firefighter Dwayne Frost, Sr. of Capitol Heights joined the Army's 82nd Airborne Division. Serving two tours in Iraq, he was awarded the Bronze Star for capturing the 7 of Hearts in 55 Most Wanted Iraqis deck of cards. Sergeant Frost was seriously wounded when a suicide bomber struck his Humvee. After many operations, his right leg below the knee could not be saved. "I don't look at my leg as a disability, I see it as a mishap I'm overcoming," Frost wanted to rejoin the fire department, and was cleared to work exterior fires and operate EMS services, after proving he could climb ladders, low crawl and even jump into his protective gear in 30 seconds. "All I want to do is get back to work, doing what I love doing," said Frost "Firefighting."[41]

Virginia

"The minute I forget to balance reality with the fantasy, I'm going back to Virginia."

Schuyler Fisk

From Thomas Jefferson to Misty of Chincoteague

Like Maryland, Virginia goes from Blue Ridge Mountains to coastal plains and the extreme ends of the state seem as removed from Washington DC as you can get. While I have driven through the state many times on my way north or south, this was my second attempt at painting in Virginia. My previous trip had taken me in from the west across the Blue Ridge Mountains near Charlottesville and Thomas Jefferson's home at Monticello. I thought there could be no better inspiration for my painting than the source of the Declaration of Independence. Rain and tornado warnings foiled my effort that time. This time I drove down the eastern shore in search of a different symbol of freedom.

Like a lot of little girls growing up in a 1950's small town, I read Misty of Chincoteague. I visited Assateague Island and saw the wild ponies when I was in high school. I was anxious to see, crossing over into Virginia 40 years later, if they were still there. When I got onto the island and pulled off the side of the road, I was rewarded with a view of a distant herd. From the children's book you imagine they are just wandering on every beach. In reality they keep their distance and are usually in the marshes and meadows peeking out from behind groves of trees. Since they would not pose, I shot some photos and chose to paint a beautiful marsh where they had been moments before. It is remarkable that a place can remain unchanged. Little girls can still read a book written over 60 years ago and find the magical place that inspired it. Thanks to Jefferson and many others who have followed him, the ponies and I are still free to roam.

Army Staff Sgt. Arthur "Bunky" Woods, Warren County, served two tours of duty in Iraq in his six years of service. As an experienced leader, Sergeant Woods often commanded his entire platoon and was involved in over 250 combat missions and over 100 escort missions. Woods was hit in the back of the neck by a sniper bullet and paralyzed from the neck down. His Platoon Captain said "His training of those 18 guys and myself is really what kept us all safe for the duration of our combat without him." Woods is enrolled in college classes and looks forward to graduating, getting married, raising a family and "living a more normal life." *Homes for Our Troops* built an adapted home for Woods so he could be more independent.[42]

Connecticut

"History formed a kind of living atmosphere here. It hovered like a pocket of quiescent air upon us. It lived in the names of roads and ponds and mountains that were the names of first-settling families..."

-Far From Home

Ron Powers

Off course in Litchfield

Before driving to Connecticut, I picked up my daughter in New York so we could visit a bit while I painted the next two days. We got off the Interstate in southern Connecticut and headed up Scenic Route 7. My aim was to find a great place to paint that would show the quiet side of Connecticut that was not just a suburb of New York. I intended to stay on Route 7 but accidentally got diverted onto 202 toward Litchfield.

Litchfield had a rich history during the Revolutionary War when it was a "safe town" The coastal areas were under constant attack by the British and most of the supplies came through Litchfield establishing it as a wealthy commercial center. In 1776, the Sons of Liberty tore down a statue of King George III in New York City. They sent the pieces to Litchfield, where the many of the town's women and children melted them into 42,000 bullets in the orchard behind Oliver Wolcott's home.

I contemplated turning around to get back on Route 7 but the road before me started to look interesting. As often happens, my favorite moments on the trip happen when I am off course. This time my accidental instincts led me to a small farm between Litchfield and Torrington that belonged to the Ryle family. I stopped to ask permission to paint on their property and talked to the father and son that were working in the barn that had caught my eye. The son was a vet of the first Gulf War and I promised to show him the resulting painting. When I was done I kept my promise and had a nice chat with him when he graciously invited me into their home. I told him about my project and promised to send him a copy.

Sgt. Jared Luce USMCR, Coventry, was severely injured when the HMMWV he was driving was blown up by a double-stacked land mine as he drove the vehicle to recover a broken down vehicle in the convoy. Jared lost both of his legs and suffered severe damage to his left hand and left eye. Jared participated in the *Christmas Can Cure* Program in New Hampshire saying he was, "looking forward to building snow forts with my three boys!" One of Jared's #1 desires is to stay in the Marine Corps Reserve and go back to school. [43]

Massachusetts

"We shall pay any price, bear any burden, meet any hardship, support any friend, oppose any foe to assure the survival and the success of liberty."

John F. Kennedy

A Berkshire Cottage

One of my purposes of getting on the back roads was to see the true nature of the country. Many areas of the country are dominated by large cities. While I love the museums, the architecture, the history and the culture of great cities like Boston, it is harder to see their true character as a visitor. I woke up in Great Barrington, Massachusetts and it was cold. For this trip we have been blessed with perfect fall weather at the peak of the foliage. Taking an early morning walk, I found that our hotel was across the street from a castle. I rushed back to the hotel to get my oil paints and bundled up. It was a private school so I had to paint from outside the gate. But it was a great subject, one befitting Massachusetts and another testament to the benefit of being open to surprises along the road.

Searles Castle has a long history beginning with how it was first designed. Mary Hopkins was the widow of railroad tycoon Mark Hopkins and inherited the castle in 1888. The richest woman in America married her designer, Edward Searles, who was 22 years her junior. Four years later, her death raised scandalous rumors about his intention, as did the will which left him everything. The railroad industry created Gilded Age resort communities like Great Barrington during the reconstruction period following the Civil War. The industrial magnates that made their fortune on the greatest period of expansion in US history had their "Berkshire cottages" like Searles Castle. Some tycoons earned their titles of "robber barons," taking advantage of trust laws to create monopolies. From the railroad wealth they invested in banks, hotel chains, and public utilities. Names like Astor, Vanderbilt, Rockefeller, and DuPont became American royalty. But they also established philanthropic foundations for generations to come. Many colleges and museums can thank Carnegie, Mellon, Frick, Guggenheim and many others who gave away their fortunes.

In 2004 Marine Lance Cpl James Crosby (Ret) of Winthrop, MA suffered a severe spinal cord injury when his truck was hit by a rocket attack. During his recovery Crosby was aided by fellow Marines who visited and organized a fundraiser. After more than 14 surgeries and months of rehabilitation, Crosby helped pass the Crosby Puller Combat Compensation Act that continued combat pay for wounded veterans while they recover. Crosby now heads the outreach crisis program, SAVE, for the MA Department of Veterans. "I believe that when I took that oath to serve my country it didn't stop the day that I was retired from the Marine Corps."[44]

Rhode Island

"My hand trembles, but my heart does not."   Stephen Hopkins

Rhode Island delegate, on signing the Declaration of Independence, July 4, 1776

Rogue's Island

Rhode Island should not have been located so far to one side of the country. It is an easy state to miss on the road through New England but one that was important to the nation's founding. I entered Rhode Island from Route 96 in Massachusetts and followed it to Route 102 in the western part of the state.

Near Coventry I found good light, fall colors and a horse barn to paint. As I began to set up by the road, the owner came out and asked me if I wanted to buy the property. She was a very nice woman who told me the horse graphic on the barn (not shown in my painting) was done by her son. As I finished, her son arrived and I explained that his artistic detail did not fit in my small painting.

We drove on to the coast at the Charlestown Breachway in the late afternoon. I took some great photos of the fishermen who lined the rock jetty, happy that I was not painting in the wind and blowing sand.

In 1636 Rev. Roger Williams was banished from Massachusetts Bay Colony for his religious views. The Narragansett Tribe gave him some land on the tip of the bay and he named it "Providence." Other dissidents followed in Warwick, Portsmouth and Newport and together they formed the colony of Rhode Island. The Puritans called it "Rogue's Island." Williams was a student of Indian languages and an advocate for their fair treatment. But by 1670, relations between the settlers and the native tribes had deteriorated and culminated in King Philip's War. When American militia destroyed the Narragansett village, the Natives retaliated by burning several Rhode Island cities including Providence. 100 years later, Rhode Island became the first British colony to declare their independence, two months before the formal Declaration of Independence.

Sgt. Brian Neuman of Portsmouth was a construction worker at the time of the 9/11 attacks. Already having served 4 years, he re-enlisted, did two tours in Afghanistan, and then volunteered for Iraq in August 2004. He was in a Bradley vehicle in a convoy when a rocket-propelled grenade burst in, took off his left arm, cut the pistol in his waistband in half and killed the interpreter sitting next to him. He retired from the Army and worked for the *Wounded Warrior Project*, launching a wounded vet hiring program at *USAA*. "I'm proud of the things I've sacrificed," he said. "September 11 changed my life: I met my wife, I'm proud I get to make sure soldiers get taken care of" "For the one thing I have to be sad about," he says, "I have a thousand things to be happy about."[45]

"Paterson lies on the valley under the Passaic Falls

Its spent waters forming the outline of his back.

He lies on his right side, head near the thunder of the water, filling his dreams!"

-Paterson   William Carlos Williams

94

A Barrel with Both Ends Open

"The Garden State" is still on the New Jersey license plate and the slogan's history dates back to 1876. A minor political figure, Abraham Browning gave a speech at the New Jersey Centennial. He said "that our Garden State is like a huge barrel, with both ends open, one of which is plucked by New York and the other by Pennsylvania." Despite 80 years and 2 gubernatorial vetoes, it became the state slogan in 1954. When I was growing up in Pennsylvania I remember being surprised when I crossed the border for my first trip to Atlantic City, to see green fields and neat little houses, not the gray urban landscape people had described as "the city." While not filled with gardens, there is still open country within 30 minutes of Newark. I had a special attachment to Atlantic City where I had my first art job during college. I drew portraits on the Old Steel Pier in the days before casinos, when there was still the diving horse and the carnival boardwalk culture. For my painting, I headed to an area near Polkville where the early morning light and shadow on a white fence caught my eye.

Originally the home of the Lenape (now called the Delaware) tribe, New Jersey was explored by Verrazzano in 1524, then settled by the Swedes and Dutch before becoming a British colony. It was New Jersey statesman William Paterson who helped devise the Great Compromise. It gave smaller states equal representation and resulted in creating two separate bodies of Congress. In the 1850's the City of Paterson became the cradle of the Industrial Revolution with power harnessed from the Passaic Falls. Agriculture had already become a less reliable source of income by the time Browning made his famous barrel speech.

When 21-year-old Cartaret native George Perez of the 82nd Airborne Division was wounded in Iraq on Sept. 14, 2003, he told the surgeons to do whatever they could to quickly return him to his unit. "I've got a lot of things to do," Perez said "I want to do as much as I can and as much as they will let me." He made his first parachute jump in December since losing his leg. He is the first 82nd Airborne paratrooper to jump with a prosthesis. Reenlisted at the time of this writing, he was awaiting for approval to be deployed with his unit.[46]

New Mexico

"New Mexico hills

Are spotted like lizards,

They sinuously glide and dissemble;

If you take a forked stick you may catch one and hold it."

-Red Earth   Alice Corbin Henderson

A Kingdom, a Province and a State

On my first trip to New Mexico I did not take my paints and that would be the last time I traveled there without them. There is something magical about the light and colors in New Mexico that makes painters want to do little else. On that first trip I mentioned that I was a painter to a campground owner and naively asked if there were a lot of painters in the area. He replied "The skies are black with them." Undaunted, I returned as one of the hoard to capture a landscape in the Pecos Wilderness.

Following Spain's conquest of the "Kingdom of New Mexico" in 1540, the native Indians were subjected to years of mistreatment as the Spaniards tried to convert their religious beliefs by suppressing their native traditions. They were also frequently enslaved in the "encomienda" system which allowed the collection of "tributes" in return for protection from military threats. Santa Fe became the capital of the Spanish colony following completion of its construction in 1610. In the Pueblo Revolt of 1680 the native people finally struck back at their overseers, burning most of Santa Fe but spared the governor's Palace. The massacre of 400 settlers caused the Spanish to retreat to Mexico. Their reign lasted until 1892 when the diverse Pueblo languages and conflict over who would occupy Santa Fe led to their defeat. Spain recaptured and maintained control until 1821 when Mexico gained its independence and New Mexico became its province.

It was then that William Becknell arrived from Missouri and established the Santa Fe Trail. The Mexican American War gave most of New Mexico, Arizona and Southern California to the United States in 1846.

> The Governor's Palace in Santa Fe, is the oldest seat of the Government in the United States

Construction of the transcontinental railroad resulted in additional land being added to New Mexico and Arizona by way of the Gadsden Purchase. New Mexico became the 47th state in 1912. It retains a diverse cultural identity with a population that is 45% Hispanic and 9% Indian. (There are no statistics for the percentage of painters.)

AF Senior Airman Michael Malarsie lost his eyesight to an IED explosion on an Afghanistan road where he had previously handed out candy to local children. A second explosion killed four of his fellow soldiers who had gone to rescue the wounded. Malarsie, of Bosque Farms, received the Purple Heart for his sacrifice, but is not feeling sorry for himself. "I thought, you know it happened; let's just move forward." said Malarsie. Six months after the explosion, Malarsie got married and was an expectant father.[47]

Arizona

"The Grand Canyon is carven deep by the master hand; it is the gulf of silence, widened in the desert; it is all time inscribing the naked rock; it is the book of earth."

- *The Road of a Naturalist*

Donald Culross Peattie

Civil and Uncivil Wars

I had driven to the Grand Canyon on a previous trip but I had not painted there. Having seen many paintings of the Grand Canyon, it seemed almost an impossible subject. Even the great paintings cannot give you the sense of time and your own insignificance that standing on the rim gives you. When I went back to paint in Arizona, it was to Scottsdale. Near Roosevelt Lake in the Tonto National Forest, the cacti were blooming in yellow, white, red and pink and the giant saguaros were magnificent. After painting on several trails, I came back into the Old Town in Scottsdale to paint a street scene.

Arizona was part of the New Mexico Territory after the Mexican American War in 1846. The Apaches at first aided the US military to end the brutal reign of the Mexicans. But when the California gold rush began, miners rushed into Arizona, infringing on Apache land and sparking renewed conflict. During the Civil War the southern part of the territory declared itself independent of the United States to join the Confederacy. Southern California Territory, sympathetic to the Confederacy, had laid the groundwork to secede and complete a Confederate route to the Pacific. In 1862 the Battle of Picacho Pass, 35 miles north of Tucson, was the westernmost battle of the Civil War. The Union captured Tucson and southern California's plan to secede never happened. At the same time, the military was also at war with the Apaches. The Apache Wars officially started when Cochise was invited to a peaceful dinner only to be charged with a crime and captured. He escaped but lost his entire family and declared war. When his successor, Geronimo, took over in 1874, the US had forced the Apaches to an inhospitable wilderness in San Carlos. Geronimo was eventually tracked down, his captors aided by Apache scouts.

Air force TSgt Matt Slaydon of Phoenix volunteered for three deployments into Iraq. He had over 200 combat missions, disarmed over 100 IEDs and destroyed over 150,000 pounds of captured enemy ordnance. In 2007, an IED that Slaydon was investigating detonated. As a result of the blast, he lost his eyesight, his dominant left arm above the elbow and suffered multiple facial fractures. But what he misses most is the job he loved to do, saving other soldiers' lives. He has now dedicated himself to earning a Doctorate in Clinical Psychology and wishes to work with active duty service members or veterans who suffer from Post Traumatic Stress Disorder.[48]

Alaska

"Beyond this, the endless mountains curving like a scimitar.

And in the querulous mind, the yearning heart, a sudden immeasurable calm."

-Autumn in the Alaska Range

Tom Sexton

When in Doubt, Go Up

It did not take long. It was my third day in Alaska and we were flying with a bush pilot from Glacier Bay to Haines and the weather was not perfect. I could not explain the calm I felt. By the following day, I got it. It was lack of worry on the level of a religious experience. Alaska surrounds you with endlessness and tension seems to flow into the vastness around you. I could not stop thinking "Everything is going to be alright."

A trip to Alaska was my Dad's 80th birthday present and since my Mother's health prevented her from going, I went in her place. Fortunately I took my paints and captured a quick landscape five years before this book idea occurred to me. Dad and I were lucky to see the peak of Denali (McKinley) which is clouded for 80% of visitors.

The first humans in Alaska migrated via the Bering Land Bridge sometime between 16,000 and 10,000 BC. By the 1700's there were regular fur traders settling in Alaska, most of them Russian. As word spread of the quality of the furs, competition increased and some traders enslaved the Aleuts to do the work for them. As the animal population declined, the Aleuts were forced to take greater risks in rougher seas to fill the growing companies' needs while growing more dependent on the Russians' barter system for survival. In two generations 80% of the Aleut population was destroyed by Old World diseases and violence. Sitka became the Russian capital of Alaska and from there the Russian Orthodox religion was spread to other regions. The missionaries had the positive effect of opposing the exploitation of the Aleuts and documenting the violence that occurred. Spanish and British traders also made settlements in the late 1700's but the Spanish gave their holdings to the US in 1819. Russia never was able to fully colonize Alaska and wanted to prevent it from falling into British hands. They sold it to the United States for $7,200,000 at the instigation of William Seward who endured great ridicule for buying what was understood to be a frozen wasteland. The discovery of gold and oil would more than vindicate him a few decades later.

Army Lt. Col. Marc Hoffmeister of Eagle River lost part of his arm during his second tour in Iraq in 2007. As part of his recovery, he credits his wife with challenging him to climb Mount McKinley. In "Operation Denali" he organized a group from *Wounded Warriors*, hand picking those with minimal climbing experience. Hoffmeister said he encourages Wounded Warriors to confront their challenges, or what he referred to as their 'personal summit.' "When in doubt, go up."[49]

Hawai'i

"E na'i wale nō 'oukou, i ke kupono 'a'ole au"

Prevail/continue my righteous deeds, they are not yet finished.

-Last words of

King Kamehameha

The Free Family

Hawaii's strategic importance as a coaling station for ships in 1860 would eventually make it a military base, a territory and finally a state. I was nine when the 50th star was added to the flag and I remember the excitement of that event. There was something special about reaching the number 50 and Hawaii seemed an exotic faraway place that everyone would want to go to. It was the stuff of dream vacations and honeymoons. Painting my 50th state gave me all the reason I needed to finally make the trip and I heard many suggestions about the best places to go. But I knew where I wanted to finish this journey and what the subject would be.

Growing up, Pearl Harbor was part of the history lesson taught in remembrances by our parents. Nowhere in Pearl Harbor is the history more powerful than at the USS Arizona Memorial. In the white shrine over the ship's remains, the 1177 names of the crew who were killed aboard the ship are engraved in white marble. The inset shows only about one fourth of the names. In reading the names, I noticed the multiples of last names. 37 sets of brothers served on the Arizona and one father and son. Thomas Augusta Free and his 18 year old son William both died that day. William was studying to be a machinist's mate like his Dad. Like most of those who served, he was at the beginning of a promising life.

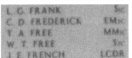

After Pearl Harbor, young men like William Free volunteered in droves. Although the draft was instituted, the volunteer lines at recruitment offices went around the block. 16 million men and women would enroll in the military by the end of the war, including my Dad.

I have asked him about his and others' eagerness to serve and willingness to sacrifice. His "That's just what we did" response was characteristic of his generation.

Dionisios Nicholas became a US citizen in Guam in 1987 when he joined the Marines. In his 23 years of service, he suffered three spinal injuries resulting in permanent nerve damage and was medically discharged from duty. As a *Mission Continues* Fellow sponsored by the Travis Manion Foundation, Nicholas worked as a National Park Service Ranger at the *USS Arizona Memorial.* Fluent in 4 languages, he now serves as a Regional Outreach Coordinator for other veterans who need assistance. [50]

Afterword

Most of us in the United States were fortunate enough to be born into this place and time and grew up taking it for granted. We went to school, learned a little history and saw our futures laid out before us like an open road. There was so much ahead of us and we expected that it would always be there.

When I began this journey as a simple painting trip, I was always eager to get over the next hill and to see the next potential scene. Sometimes I pulled over to take a picture, only to find that the best view was behind me. I learned to slow down and look back more often. I learned to turn around and explore a side road or follow a sign. That was where I found the hidden treasures of America. I left many states with regret that weather or my self-imposed schedule prevented me from taking more time.

Our history and our cultural threads run through every state and region. Like the small roads and unincorporated towns, they do not all show up on the map. The shining moments and dismal failures of our history are all there, too. But they are not stories that can be told in a paragraph or grasped from a single source. My paintings offer a glimpse of the everyday stories to be discovered and they are by no means intended to be the whole story. My writing of history is only intended to be an introduction and my facts are as I understood them. There is much history that will forever remain disputed. If this book causes someone to investigate further, that is a good outcome.

We should always look back.

Above all, I've learned that many people sacrificed to give us what we don't even think about. In writing about the history of the United States, I am not failing to recognize that there were cultures here before us. They, like us, had their triumphs and failures, as well as their conflicts with each other. Our scars remind us of where we have been and whose shoulders we stand on.

We should always look around us.

There are those among us who are still sacrificing to protect us: heroes worthy of books and those quiet everyday heroes we will never know of. And there are those who go to work each day and keep everything running. They filled the potholes, fixed flat tires and worked at the gas stations and restaurants along the road.

We should always look forward.

Whether our ancestors came to this land by choice or by force, independence swas in their blood. If freedom was denied them, they desired it more and fought for it for their children. We inherited the Land of the Free and have their independent streak within us. We look down the road and pass the gift of freedom on to our children.

BIBLIOGRAPHY AND DONATION WEBSITES

1. Used with permission of Bill Knight; *The Way We Get By:* Thewaywegetbymovie.com   www.themainetroopgreeters.com
2. Used with permission of CD Young; US Paralympics   www.usparalympics.org
3. Used with permission of M. Andrade; Native American News Blog 12/28/2008.
4. Used with permission of Kevin Workman; Liberty Lodge Outfitters   www.libertylodgeoutfitters.com
5. Flight93MemorialSFB.com; www.honorflight93.org; www.nps.gov/flni   www.honorflight93.org
6. Achilles Track Club Freedom Team; Amputee Coalition of America   www. achillesinternational.org
7. Charlotte Motor Speedway newsletter 9/16/2010   www.amputee-coalition.org
8. Air Force News (www.af.mil), Army News (www.army.mil)   www.safariclubfoundation.org
9. Photo credit: US Paralympics; St Petersburg Times, John Romano, 5/26/08   www.usparalympics.org
10. Wheelers for the Wounded   www.wheelersforthewounded.org
11. US Army (www.army.mil); Operation Home Front   www.operationhomefront.net
12. Iraq and Afghanistan Veterans of America, IAVA   www.IAVA.org
13. A Soldier's Courage, Janis Galatas; Used with permission of Janis Galatas; Photo: Project Healing Waters   www.projecthealingwaters.org
14. Oregon Active; Homes for Our Troops; VetsForVictory.com; Photo credit: Military Times   www.oregonactive.com
15. Friends of American Heroes; Safari Club International Foundation   www.friendsofamericanheroes.org
16. The Mission Continues; Big Brothers Big Sisters   www.bbbs.org
17. Franchise Times March 2007 Nancy Weingartner; USA Today Tom Vanden Brook 11/23/2004;   www.themissioncontinues.org
    Little Caesars Veterans Program (http://franchise.littlecaesars.com/VeteransProgram/tabid/76/Default.aspx)
18. Daniel Gilyeat (www.CombatVeteransforCongress.org); Operation Payback   www.operationpayback.org
19. Nebraska State Historical Society (www.nebraskahistory.org)   www.vetsforvictory.org
20. Disabled American Veterans   www.dav.org
21. American Patriot Program; War on Terror News   www.americanpatriotprogram.kk5.org
22. LeeAlley.com; University of Wyoming (www.uwyo.edu); Mobile Riverine Force Association   www.mrfa.org
23. Project Healing Waters (www.projecthealingwaters.org); Any Soldier (www.anysoldier.com)   www.anysoldier.com
24. Canine companions for Independence; Crane Aerospace & Electronics   www.caninecompanions.org
25. Nish.org; Skookum Ability One Program   www.nish.org; www.skookum.org
26. Wounded Warrior Project; Mail Tribune, Paul Fattig, May 9, 2010   www.woundedwarriorproject.org
27. Coalition for Iraq and Afghanistan Veterans; American Pain Foundation   www.painfoundation.org
28. Ezra Realty (www.ezrarealty.com/craigfitzgerald.php); Las Vegas Review-Journal   www.coalitionforveterans.org
29. Homes for Our Troops   www.Homesforourtroops.org
30. Wall Street Warfighters Foundation; Wounded Warrior Disabled Sports Project   www.wallstreetwarfighters.org
31. Folds of Honor, Vets for Victory   www.foldsof honor.com
32. Support Dogs Inc.; Southeast Missourian, Bridget Dicosmo, 9/04/09   www.supportdogs.org
33. Dept of Defense; Photo credit: Donna Miles   www.neads.org
34. Team River Runner; Wounded Warrior Project; The Mission Continues   www.teamriverrunner.org
35. Beating the Odds Foundation; www.rockybleier.com; photo: Pittsburgh Steelers   www.beatingtheodds.com
36. Disabled Sports USA   www.DSUSA.org
37. Building Homes for Heroes   www.buildinghomesforheroes.com
38. Operation Proper Exit, Troops First Foundation; USO   www.troopsfirstfoundation.org
39. Veterans of Valor   www.veteransofvalor.org
40. Homes for Our Troops; Paralyzed Veterans of America   www.pva.org
41. Firefighter Nation, Mark Brady, 8/17/ 2010; Prince George's County Fire and EMS Department, Jen   www.firefighternation.com
    McClelland photo

42.	Homes for Our Troops; WCR Photos/Roger Bianchini	www.christmascancure.org
43.	Christmas Can Cure; Homes for Our Troops	www.mass.gov (keyword Save Team)
44.	MA Statewide Advocacy for Veterans Empowerment; Paralyzed Veterans of America	www.uso.org
45.	US Army (www.army.mil); USAA, Photo by Gerry J. Gilmore	www.vfw.org
46.	El Boricua (www.elboricua.com); VFW	www.webofsupport.com
47.	Defense Dept., Air Force Times	www.fisherhouse.org
48.	Air Force (www.af.mil)	www.theveteranscolaition.org
49.	Veterans Coalition; United States Army, Jessica Maxwell, Public Affairs Specialist	www.pacifichistoryparks.org
50.	The Mission Continues; Arizona Memorial	

The Special Operations Warrior Foundation provides full scholarship grants and educational and family counseling to the surviving children of special operations personnel who die in operational or training missions and immediate financial assistance to severely wounded special operations personnel and their families. SOWF is a 4 star rated charity for efficiently managing its financing. To donate, please visit www.specialops.org or mail your donation to:

**Special Operations Warrior Foundation
P.O. Box 13483
Tampa, FL 33681-3483**

Special Thanks to: All our veterans and their families, the news media who feature our veterans' stories, the writers and poets for their words about the states, the good people of every state who shared their history and help, and the charitable organizations for sharing their information and bios.
Thank you, Roger, for seeing me off, welcoming me back and taking the journey with me.